Eucalypts for E

A Guide to the Identificati
found in South-eastern Australia

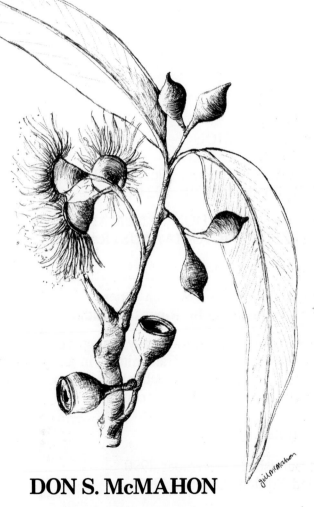

DON S. McMAHON

Illustrations by
JILL McMAHON

Published by:
DON S. McMAHON
55 VICTORIA PARADE
FITZROY, VICTORIA, 3065, AUSTRALIA
TELEPHONE: (03) 417 2927

Printing Consultant - Warren Jones
Printed in Australia by Ringwood Litho

ISBN 0 646 02372 1

First published, December 1990
Second Edition, October 1992

Complete book printed on Recycled paper

ACKNOWLEDGMENTS

Without my wife Marlene's continual involvement, this book could not have happened. Not only did she provide constant moral support, but also was physically involved in every step of its development. Without complaint she accompanied me on numerous expeditions over the changing terrain of South-east Australia. Trips by car, train, plane and even boat. Long hikes in remote desert places or steep climbs in rugged mountains, often with only a compass and map as guide.

My two daughters Mandy and Jill must take the credit for the initial interest in Eucalypts. It started with their "Tree Honour" and has not ceased since. I am especially grateful to Jill for drawing the collection of buds and nuts that have accumulated over the years.

I am also indebted to the many experts who have supplied me with the information that was required for the book ie. where a good example of a species is to be found - what it looks like when I get there - characteristics of newly described species - reading my manuscripts and making helpful suggestions. Particularly, I would like to thank Ken Hill of the National Herbarium of New South Wales, Kevin Rule of Melbourne and David Albrecht from the National Herbarium of Victoria. Without them this book would not have happened. Others who have helped are Mike Crisp of the Australian National Botanic Gardens, Canberra, Jennifer Chappill formerly of the School of Botany, University of Melbourne, Pauline Ladiges of the School of Botany, University of Melbourne. I also wish to thank the many Forestry and National Park Rangers who have accommodated my wishes and guided my path throughout Forests and National Parks of the four States of South-east Australia.

The second of edition of 'Eucalypts for Enthusiasts' is a modification of the first edition. The same basic structure remains; however, three major modifications have been made with the assistance of the book `Flora of New South Wales'. These include the addition of a number of species described since the writing of the first edition; an upgrading of the taxonomy; and increased detail on the geographical distribution of the species.

Finally I would like to thank the book itself, not only for providing a fruitful hobby, but for being a teacher. Through it I have learnt the basic skills of bush walking, mountain climbing, map reading, four-wheel driving, camping, preserving biological specimens, collecting information and word processing. I hope you, the reader can gain a part of the reward that this book has brought to my family and me.

INTRODUCTION

The purpose of this book is to provide a key to be used in the identification of the eucalypts of South-eastern Australia. The key used is not a standard two choice key; instead a multi-choice key has been devised in order to simplify and reduce the number of questions to be answered when following through the identification process. Just under three hundred eucalypts can be identified using the key. They are arranged in order according to their classification.

The key places the species into groups. Few botanical names are used for the groups because botanists have not, as yet, agreed upon a uniform naming system. For the purpose of identifying the groups common names are used (for example, `stringybark'). In the cases where no common group name exists, a common feature is used as the identifying name (for example, `double-capped eucalypts'). When there is no common name or suitable common feature with which to name a group, an Anglicised form of the Pryor and Johnson terminology is used (for example, `subseries Viminalinae' becomes `Manna Gums and Others'). All published species of eucalypts found in South-eastern Australia including the rare and isolated ones can be identified using the key. Several unpublished species are also included. These are designated in the text as E. species.

The major limitation of this key is that the identification process relies heavily upon the buds, nuts and juvenile leaves. These may not always be found. It is usual in books written for amateur botanists, to use the more easily found characters of bark, form of the tree and the adult leaves as a starting point for an identification key. Unfortunately these more easily found characteristics are not varied enough between species or constant enough within species to differentiate a large number of species. In many cases it is better to use the more difficult to find, but more accurate features. This may mean experimentation and the use of common sense to complete the identification.

It should be remembered that the key can only be used for eucalypts native to South- eastern Australia. Thus it will not be appropriate for garden species growing in south-eastern Australia whose origins are in other regions of Australia.

He made each different from the norm.
In vast creative glee,
He carved in every shape and form:
The eucalyptus tree.
He knew He'd spread across the land,
Wherever plant would grow,
From driest, hottest desert sands,
To frozen fields of snow.
From highest, steepest mountain peak,
To hidden rocky crypt:
Enthusiasts - the ones who seek
The unique eucalypt.

CHAPTER 1

THE OPERCULUM SCAR

Before attempting the key a high proficiency must first be gained in identification of the operculum scar. This can only be acquired with practice on known species.

Requirements for scar identification (see page 20)
1. Only fresh buds can be used. The scar is lost with drying and browning of the buds.

2. Examine several buds from the same tree or species.

3. A x10 or x20 hand lens must be used. The scar cannot be confidently identified by the naked eye. If wearing glasses the lens is placed on the glass. If not wearing glasses it is placed at an equivalent distance from the eye. The bud is placed about 1 cm. from the lens. The accommodation of the eye is relaxed and the bud is moved backwards and forwards until it comes into focus.

4. Always examine the bud in a bright light. Sun light is the best, but take care that your hat does not shade the specimen.

5. Examine the bud carefully from the tip of the operculum to the base of the hypanthium.

What the scar looks like. See page 20.
1. It is usually found encircling the bud at or near to the widest point of the bud. In four species it is found near the apex of the operculum.

2. It is seen as a fine ragged line of brown or grey, dead tissue. There may be breaks in the line. It can even look like a series of dots. When at the apex it may be a circle about the apex or a cap of dead brown tissue over the apex.

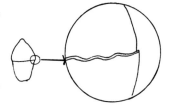

3. There is frequently a small sharp step at the line of the scar with the operculum being a little narrower than the hypanthium. It sometimes appears as a sharp edged groove.

When no scar is present-
1. There is no irregular ring of brown or grey tissue.
2. There is no step around the bud.
3. There is no break in the surface markings on the bud.
4. There is no cap of dead tissue over the apex.
5. A colour change between the operculum and hypanthium does not necessarily indicate a scar.
6. A slight smooth depressed ring between the hypanthium and the operculum does not indicate a scar.
7. A ring of discolouration does not indicate a scar.

Cautions and advice in scar identification.
1. The scar cannot be identified in dried, pressed or herbarium specimens.

2. In very young, double capped buds the outer operculum may not have yet separated. Thus scarred buds will appear non-scarred. If only very young small buds are available use the largest. If just the largest ones are scarred then the bud is scarred. If not scrape a thumb nail at the junction of the operculum and hypanthium and if it is double capped the outer operculum will come off leaving a green inner operculum.

3. In several non-scarred species (Bloodwoods and Boxes) just prior to flowering, the outer operculum may separate several days before the inner operculum. Thus a small percentage of buds may appear scarred. Keeping this fact in mind is usually enough to prevent calling a non-scarred species scarred.

4. Just before the flowering of single-capped buds, a grey or brown line often develops between the operculum and the hypanthium. Under magnification there is no jagged edge or sharp step; thus it is not scarred.

5. If no buds can be found, be prepared to search many trees and the ground under many trees. Frequently buds can be found out of season. As a last resort work through the key twice, for scarred and non-scarred. The bud is vital for the identification of an unfamiliar tree, even for the expert.

6. It is fairly unusual in the bush not to find any buds. The most frequent species in which they may not be found are the Paper-fruited Bloodwoods, Woody-fruited Bloodwoods, Ironbarks and Boxes. All these groups of species are described in the first step of the key and will be identified if the key is worked through for both scarred and non-scarred buds. Only the Ironbarks are not adequately described by the first step of the key. With their characteristic bark, however, they can readily be identified, without the buds, as belonging to the Ironbark group. Unfortunately it is not possible even for experts to confidently identify an Ironbark species, without the buds.

7. When the scar has been identified you will find it reasonably easy to place the species into its major subgenera. From that point on it is usually straight forward to identify the species correctly.

8. The advantage of starting with the buds instead of the bark or the size and shape of the tree, is that even though they are sometimes hard to find, the characteristics are consistent within species.

CHAPTER 1

How to use the key

The key begins on page 25 of this book. For each step of the key there may be more than one choice. Each step is indented and numbered.

For example:
1 **Juvenile leaves** ovate.
    2 **Adult leaves** ovate, green.

    2 **Adult leaves** ovate, glaucous.

    2 **Adult leaves** lanceolate, glaucous.

1 **Juvenile leaves** lanceolate.
    2 **Adult leaves** lanceolate, green.
        3 **Buds** in threes.

        3 **Buds** in sevens.

Step 1: The species is identified according to the characteristic labelled with a number one (using the above example, the juvenile leaves would be identified). A choice is made between all the number one characteristics.

Step 2: A choice is made between those characteristics labelled with a two (for example, adult leaves), contingent upon the choice made in step one.
    If the features needed in step one cannot be found, (for example, if there are no juvenile leaves) it is often possible to continue with the key by omitting step one and selecting from all the step two choices (that is, identifying according the to adult leaves).

Step 3: and proceeding steps: The choices continue within each step until the species is identified.
    When a page number is given, the key is continued on that page.

As a final step of the key, the identified species are presented in closely related groups with a summary of group characteristics.

For some species when it is known that an important identifying characteristic can vary between species, both variants have been included in the key.

It is advisable to have a basic knowledge of the method used in the key before expecting it to reliably come up with the correct species. In fact the best results are only gained with some basic knowledge of the characteristics of most species. It must be emphasised that if the key appears to come to an end without identification, it is necessary to start from the beginning and rework the key. Always keep in mind the possibility of a hybrid.

CHAPTER 1

TERMINOLOGY

South-east Australia includes New South Wales, Victoria, Tasmania and south-east of South Australia, south-east of a line from Broken Hill to Ceduna. The Australian Capital Territory is included with New South Wales.

The **Mallee region** is New South Wales to the west of the Newell Highway, Victoria to the west of a line from east of Bendigo to the west of the Grampians to Portland and including all of South Australia.

The geographic features are given in the broadest terms only and no maps are provided. These features are not given to find where an unknown species grows. Only enough information is given to confirm the identity of a species. In each step of the key the state where the species are found is identified by the abbreviations NSW, VIC, SA and TAS. In the final step any other state or territory where the particular species is found is identified by the abbreviations Q, NT and WA.

HABIT

mallee	-	multi-stemmed bush
small trees	-	up to 10 m
medium sized trees	-	10 m to 30 m
tall trees	-	30 m to 60 m
very tall trees	-	over 60 m

BARK

Gum bark The bark peels off in sheets or strips on a regular basis leaving a clean, relatively smooth surface.
>It may strip off in ribbons.
>It may come off in plates.
>It may have scribbles. These are lines left
>by insects burrowing in the bark.
>It may have a powdery surface.
>It may be matt ie. dull and rough.

The common colours are white, grey, green, yellow or orange.

Rough bark The old bark remains for many years. As the tree grows the bark splits and cracks. Old surface bark may flake off.

Appearance of rough bark
Extent of rough bark
Unless otherwise stated gum bark extends nearly to, or fully to the ground and rough bark to the small branches.

Partial bark The rough bark extends a variable distance up the trunk or even to the large branches.

Basal bark The rough bark covers the lower part of the trunk only.

The common Colours of the bark may be grey, black, brown or yellow.

Pattern of cracks
Furrowed	-	They are longitudinal.
Tessellated	-	They are longitudinal and horizontal.
Lattice	-	They are cris-crossing.

Degree of roughness
Fine	-	The patterns visible on close inspection.
Coarse	-	The pattern is visible from a distance.
Craggy	-	The roughness is visible whenever tree trunk is visible.

Feel of bark
Texture
Hard	-	It is very difficult to break.
Firm	-	It is moderately hard to break.
Spongy	-	It is easily compressed.

How bark comes off the tree
Long fibres	-	It peels in long strips.
Short fibres	-	It peels in medium length strips.
Flakes	-	It peels in thin small sheets or is papery.
Plates	-	It comes off in firm large sheets.
Chunks	-	It comes off in thick spongy pieces.

Oil glands in the bark
The bark of most of the Oily-barks when viewed with magnification show oil glands. The young bark of the Scent-barks when crushed will smell of eucalyptus oil.

Types of rough bark
Stringybark
It is a coarse furrowed bark that pulls off in long strips, is spongy textured and grey or brown coloured. All Stringybarks except the two Grampians Gums and E. deuaensis (Mongamulla mallee) are fully barked with classical stringybark. Trees that are not Stringybarks but have similar bark: (The bark is usually less furrowed with shorter fibres.)

> E. baileyana (Bailey's Stringybark)
> E. chapmaniana (Bogong Gum)
> The False Stringybarks of the Oily-barks
> The White Mahoganies
> The Blackbutts - partial barked.
> E. delegatensis (Alpine Ash) - partial barked.
> E. tasmaniensis (Gum -top Stringybark)
> E. fastigata (Brown Barrel)
> E. consideniana (Yertchuk) - more peppermint like.

Trees which may be confused even though they are much more spongy and much shorter fibres.

> The Red Mahoganies
> The Scent barks

Peppermint

It is a fine furrowed to latticed bark that pulls off in short strips, is firm or spongy in texture and grey in colour.
Approximately half the Peppermints have peppermint bark.
Trees that are not peppermints but have similar bark.
- E. regnans (Mountain Ash)
- E. piperita (Sydney Peppermint)
- E. andrewsii (New England Blackbutt)
- E. campanulata (New England Blackbutt
- E. olida - a little more stringy.
- E. consideniana (Yertchuk) - a little more stringy.

Box

It is a fine furrowed to tessellated bark which comes off in firm crumbly flakes and has patches of different grey.
All boxes except E. dawsonii (Slaty Box), E. polyanthemos ssp. polyanthemos (Red Box), E. fasciculosa (Pink Gum) and several mallee boxes show at least some box bark.
Trees that are not boxes but have similar bark:
- E. longifolia (Woollybutt)
- Several Divided-cotyledons
- E. morrisii (Grey Mallee)
- The False Boxes of the Oily-barks
- E. remota (Kangaroo Island Mallee)

Compact

It is a fine furrowed and hard bark which is coloured grey to black. It is found on the Black Peppermints and on the lower trunk of several ashes, gums and mallees.

Ironbark

It is a coarse to craggy and hard bark which is grey to black. Only two Ironbarks, E. leucoxylon (Yellow Gum) and E. Petiolaris (Eyre Peninsula Blue Gum), does not have ironbark and only one species, E. sieberi (Silvertop Ash), has similar bark but is not an Ironbark.

Bloodwood

It is a coarse tessellated bark that pulls off in chunks and is spongy textured.
All the Bloodwoods have bloodwood bark.
Only E. robusta (Swamp Mahogany) has similar bark but is not a Bloodwood.

Mahogany

It is a coarse furrowed bark that pulls off in elongated, spongy chunks.
E. botryoides (Southern Mahogany) and the Red Mahoganies have mahogany bark.

Plate bark

It is a course furrowed to tessellated bark that pulls off in firm plates. It is found at the base of a number of gums.

Gum
E. globulus
Blue Gum

Scribbles
E. signata
Scribbly Gum

Stringybark
E. globoidea
White Stringybark

Peppermint
E. radiata
Narrow leaf
Peppermint

Box
E. microcarpa
Grey Box

Compact
E. smithii
Gully Gum

Ironbark
E. sideroxylon
Red Ironbark

Bloodwood
E. intermedia
Pink Bloodwood

Mahogany
E. botryoides
Southern Mahogany

LEAVES

The features in these illustrations apply to both adult and juvenile leaves.

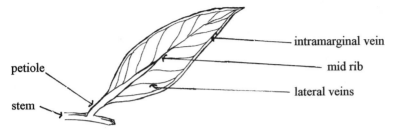

petiole

stem

intramarginal vein

mid rib

lateral veins

Attachment

petiolate - having a short petiole
attached to the leaf stem.

or

Sessile - no petiole. ie. the leaf
attached directly to the stem.

Arrangement

Alternate - leaves stepwise.

or

Opposite - leaves in pairs.

Size

As most leaves are 5 to 20 cm long, the size will only be mentioned in the text if
it is different from this or significant for the identification.

Shape

orbicular	length to width ratio about	1	:	1
ovate	length to width ratio about	2	:	1
broad-lanceolate	length to width ratio about	4	:	1
lanceolate	length to width ratio about	7	:	1
narrow-lanceolate	length to width ratio about	10	:	1
linear	length to width ratio greater than	12	:	1

Other features
Connate

Two opposite leaves are joined around the stem.
Found strongly in the juvenile leaves of:
E. sturgissiana (Ettrema Mallee)
E. perriniana (Spinning gum)
E. leucoxylon (Yellow gum, Melbourne form)
Found moderately in the juvenile leaves of:
E. risdonii (Risdon Peppermint)
E. tenuiramis (Silver Peppermint)
Found occasionally in the juvenile leaves of:
E. leucoxylon (ssp. connata and pruinosa) (Yellow gums)
E. dives (Broad-leaved Peppermint)

Peltate

The stem attaches to the
under side of the leaf.
Found occasionally in the juvenile
leaves of the Bloodwoods.

Falcate

The leaf is curved.
Strongly developed in the adult leaves
of the Single-capped Eucalypts.

Oblique

The leaf edges extend up different
lengths on each side of the petiole.
Strongly developed in adult leaves of
many of the Single-capped Eucalypts.

Undulate

The leaf has a wavy edge
when viewed from side.
Strongly developed in the Swamp Gums.

Crenulate

The leaf has an irregular edge.
Found in the juvenile leaves of
a number of species of Oily-barks
Also to a lesser extent in the adult
leaves of the Tasmanian Yellow Gums.

Denticulate

The leaf edge has pointed projections.
Found in the adult leaves of:
E. quadrangulata (White Topped Box)
E. denticulata (Errinundra Gum)

Cordate

The leaf is heart shaped.
Found in the juvenile leaves of
several species.

Colour

green
glaucous - blue-green to blue-grey with white waxy surface.
blue or grey
glossy, semi-glossy or dull

Concolourous - It is the same colour on each surface.
Discolourous - It is a different colour on each surface.
Discolourous adult leaves are found in :
The Red Bloodwoods except E. opaca
E. baileyana (Bailey's Stringybark)
E. microcorys (Tallowwood)
Eastern Blue Gums, Mahoganies and Grey Gums
E. cladocalyx (Sugar Gum)
E. angophoroides (Apple-topped Box)
E. rummeryi (Steel Box)
E. hypostomatica
E. paniculata (Grey ironbark)(two subspecies)
E. fergusonii (two subspecies)
E. placita
E. fusiformis
E. acmenoides (White Mahogany)
E. apothalassica (Inland White Mahogany)
E. muelleriana (Yellow Stringybark)

Slightly or sometimes discolourous in:
E. michaeliana (Brittle Gum)
E. brookeriana (Brooker Gum)
E. ancophila
The White Stringybarks

Texture

The surface may be smooth or rough.
The juvenile leaves are rough in:
The Paper-fruited Bloodwoods
The Woody-fruited Bloodwoods
E. baileyana (Bailey's Stringybark)
The true Stringybarks

The leaf may be leathery ie. thick.

Position

Vertical: the leaf is below the petiole.
Most adult and some juvenile leaves especially the Ashes are vertical.

Horizontal: one surface up and the other down.
Most juvenile and discolourous adult leaves are horizontal

Erect: the leaf is above the petiole.
The mallee ashes are of this type.

Venation

Lateral veins are often not visible in narrow leaves. Most species of south-east Australia have the lateral veins at approximately to 45 degrees to the mid rib. Venation will only be mentioned when they varies from this form.
Found in the leaves of:
White Mahoganies
All the Double-capped Eucalypts except the Mahoganies and Grey Gums.

Transverse venation: There are many side veins making an angle greater than 45 degrees to the mid rib and parallel to each other. The intramarginal vein is near the edge.
Found in adult leaves of:
The Paper-fruited Bloodwoods
The Woody-fruited Bloodwoods
E. baileyana (Bailey's Stringybark)
The Transverse-veins

Acute venation: There are few side veins making an acute angle to mid rib. The intramarginal vein is remote from the edge.
Found in adult leaves of:
All the Single Capped Eucalypts except the White Mahoganies, the Snow Gums (White Sallies) and most Black Sallies.
Several of the Boxes.

Parallel venation:
The lateral veins run parallel to the mid rib.
Found in the Snow Gums (White Sallies) and most Black Sallies.

Stomata

Under magnification with reflected light, small openings are visible on the leaf surface.

Oil Glands in the pith.

Stripping the petiole of a leaf off a young branch will expose a spongy pith in the centre of the branch. If the pith is viewed with a hand lens oil glands if present are visible as oval depressions. They are found in all species of the Ribbed-Mallees and in E. trivalvis (Victoria Springs Mallee).

Oil Glands in the leaf

Small clear dots seen when the leaf is held up to a bright light.

Leaf Phases

Cotyledons are the first two leaves that emerge from the seed. In the Divided-cotyledons they are divided into four. In all other species the are either not divided or partially divided into a bean shape.

Seedling leaves are the first two or three leaves following the cotyledons. They are usually opposite. By the time the young tree is able to be identified they are usually not seen.

Juvenile leaves are the leaves seen on young plants or on coppice growth. They can be arranged in the following ways.

Alternate and petiolate. The first two or three leaves may be opposite and sessile but after that they are stepwise.

Sub-opposite and shortly petiolate. The leaves are not quite opposite and have short petioles.

Opposite and sessile. The paired leaves persist for many pairs and are frequently found on both young and even adult trees.

Intermediate leaves are similar to adult leaves but are broader and may show some juvenile characteristics like crenulate edges.

Adult leaves are on mature trees. They are usually alternate, petiolate and broad lanceolate or narrower. Unless otherwise stated, adult leaves are assumed to be alternate and petiolate.

Some species mature in the juvenile stage and never or rarely form adult leaves. Persistent opposite and sessile juvenile leaves (matures with opposite umbels):
E. gillii (Curly Mallee)
E. parvula (Small-leaved Gum)
E. recurva
E. crenulata (Victorian Silver Gum)
E. vernicosa (Varnished Gum)
E. cordata (Heart-leaved Silver Gum)
E. pulverulenta (Silver-leaved Mountain Gum)
The False Stringybarks
E. melanophloia (Silver-leaved Ironbark)
E. risdonii (Risdon Gum)

Persistent alternate and petiolate juvenile leaves (ovate or wider):
E. deanei (Round-leaved Gum)
E. brunnea (Round-leaved Gum)
E. camphora (Mountain Swamp Gum)
E. populnea (Bimble Box)
E. polyanthemos (Red Box)(two subspecies)
E. bauerana (blue Box)
E. magnificata (Blue Box)
E. caleyi (Caley's Ironbark) (two subspecies)

INFLORESCENCES
The flower buds, flowers and fruit are arranged in structures called **inflorescences**.

An **umbel** is a single cluster of buds, flowers or fruit. The number per umbel may be one, three, seven, or more than seven (in some species there are over twenty). The arrangement of the inflorescences are best seen in the bud stage.

There is one bud per umbel in two species only:
> E. globulus (Tasmanian Blue Gum)
> E. vernicosa (varnished Gum)

There are three buds per umbel in:
> E. longifolia (Woollybutt)
> E. cosmophylla (Cup Gum)
> E. morrisii (Grey Mallee)
> less than half of the Oily-bark group
> E. tricarpa (Red Ironbark)
> E. leucoxylon (Yellow Gum)
> E. codonocarpa (Bell-fruited Mallee)
> E. triflora (pigeon House Ash)

Three buds per umbel are some times found in:
> E. tessellaris (Carbeen)
> The Spotted Gums
> E. scias (Large-fruited Red Mahoganies) (three subspecies)
> E. concinna (Victoria Desert Mallee)
> E. costata (Ridge-fruited Mallee)
> E. angulosa (Ridge-fruited Mallee)
> E. flindersii (South Australian Grey Mallee)
> E. species (South Gippsland Blue Gum)
> E. coccifera (Tasmanian Snow Gum)

The **Peduncle** is the common peduncle
stem for the cluster.
It is **Pedunculate**
when present
and **Non pedunculate**
when absent.

pedicel

leaf

The **Pedicel** is the stem between the peduncle and the bud.

> **Pedicellate**
> The pedicel is present.

> **Sessile**
> The pedicel is absent.

> **sub-sessile**
> The pedicel is very short.

18

CHAPTER 1

Arrangement   - Axillary and simple

  The umbels are arranged along the
stem with one for each leaf node.
They do not extend along the
branch beyond the last leaf.

- Axillary and paired

There are two umbels per leaf node
each with its own peduncle. They do
not extend along the branch beyond
the last leaf.
They are found in three species only:
E. squamosa ((Scaly Bark)
E. regnans (Mountain Ash)
E. fastigata (Brown Barrel)

- Axillary and compound

There is a large cluster for each
leaf node. The peduncles are branched.
They do not extend along the branch
beyond the last leaf.
They are found in two species only:
E. tessellaris ((Carbeen)
E. michaeliana (Hillgrove Gum)
In a number of the Boxes, Ironbarks
and Bloodwoods they can be combined
with terminal and compound buds.

- Terminal and compound

Most of the buds are arranged as
a large cluster at the end of the
stem beyond the last leaf.
The peduncles are branched.
They are found in:
The Non scarred Woody Fruited
Bloodwoods
The Scarred Ironbarks
Many of the Boxes

In several species which are normally axillary, the arrangement appears
terminal. This occurs if the leaves at the end of the stem are missing.
This can occur in:
The Grey Gums
E. cladocalyx (Sugar Gum)
E. viridis (Green Mallee)
E. melliodora (Yellow Box)
The White Mahoganies
If there is doubt whether a species is axillary and simple or terminal and
compound be prepared to work through the key twice. In practice a mistake is
quickly corrected.

CHAPTER 1

FLOWER BUDS

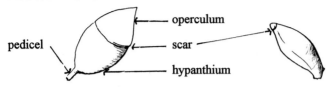

The hypanthium is the part of the bud towards the stem which remains after flowering and contains the developing seeds.

The operculum is the part of the bud which comes off as the flower opens. If there is no operculum ie. the flower opens with sepals and petals, then it is not a eucalypt.

The operculum scar, when present, is along the line of junction between the hypanthium and operculum and shows the line where the outer operculum has earlier dropped off. Page six has instruction on the identification of the operculum scar.

The apex scar, when present circles the apex of the bud or dead tissue covers the tip of the bud. It is formed by incomplete separation of the outer operculum in:
      E. benthamii (Nepean River Gum)
      E. denticulata (Errinundra Gum)
      E. Sturgissiana (Ettrema Mallee)

It is also formed by incomplete sepal formation in:
      E. baileyana (Bailey's Stringybark)

The bud may be **pedicellate, sessile** or **subsessile** (see the inflorescences. page 18)

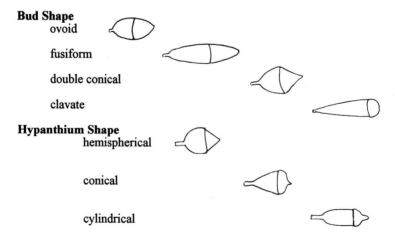

Bud Shape
    ovoid

    fusiform

    double conical

    clavate

Hypanthium Shape
    hemispherical

    conical

    cylindrical

Operculum shape
flat

hemispherical

conical
low - shorter than wide

high - longer than wide

horned - length two and a
half times longer than width.

beaked

warty

Angular - with several ridges (often appearing square in cross section)
Ribbed - with many ridges
Colour - may be green or glaucous (white waxy surface)

Anther attachment
versatile - The filament comes
to a point so that the anther
can move.
or
adnate - The filament has a
wide attachment so that the
anther cannot move

shape   oblong

or

reniform

or

globular

Staminodes   outer stamens have no anthers

21

CHAPTER 1

FRUIT

The arrangement, pedicels, peduncles are usually the same as with the buds.

The Rim   is the line where the stamens were attached.
When the disc is raised it is a line.
When the disc is depressed it is an actual rim and
can be thin (ie. less than about 1 mm.) or it can be thick
(ie. greater than about 1 mm.)

The Disc   is the part of the fruit between the rim and valves.
It may be:

raised

flat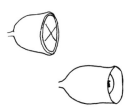

depressed

The Valves are triangular structures formed by the opening of the fruit.

There are usually 3 to 5 but may be 6. No mention will be made in the text
if the discs is depressed and the valves do not project beyond the rim.
They may be:

flat

exsert

Size   very large length or width   > 2 cm
large   length or width   1-2 cm
medium   length or width   0.6-1 cm
small   length or width   < 0.6 cm
Only maximum sizes are listed in the text.

Colour is green, brown
or glaucous (white waxy surface).

The disc may be red.

Shape   conical

hemispherical

cupular (cup shaped)

pyriform (pear shaped)

cylindrical

ovoid (barrel shaped)

campanulate (bell shaped)

urceolate (urn shaped)

globular (spherical) with ascending
disc

globular (spherical) with flat or descending
disc

compressed - flattened sides where pressing
on the adjacent fruit

angular - several ridges on the fruit (often square
in cross section) ribbed - many ridges on the fruit

CHAPTER 2 DIVISION OF EUCALYPTS

The Eucalypts of South-eastern Australia are divided into Subgenera.
They can be divided into four groups.

BLOODWOODS Page 27
Paper-fruited Bloodwoods (SUBGENUS BLAKELLA)
Woody-fruited Bloodwoods (SUBGENUS CORYMBIA)
Each bud has two **opercula**. In most species they both remain until just before
flowering, thus there is no operculum scar. In two species E. tessellaris (carbeen) and
E. eximia (Yellow Bloodwood) the outer opercula comes in early development. In
these species an operculum scar is present. Microscopic examination of a number of
species show the inner opercula breaking into petals.
The **anthers** are oblong and versatile.
The **seeds** are large and may have wing like extensions.

SEPALLED EUCALYPTS page 30
E. baileyana (SUBGENUS EUDESMIA)
E. microcorys (SUBGENUS NOTHOCALYPTUS)
This group of eucalypts are characterised by having some evidence of separate sepals.
Only two species are found in South-east Australia and they are not closely related. In
E. baileyana (Bailey's Stringybark) the sepals appear as a scar around the apex of the
operculum.
The **anthers** are oblong and versatile.
In E. microcorys (Tallowwood) the partial sepal formation is seen as a cross on the
apex of the operculum.
The **anthers** are reniform and versatile.

DOUBLE-CAPPED EUCALYPTS (SUBGENUS SYMPHYOMYRTUS) page 31
The buds have two **opercula**. In most species the outer operculum comes off in the
early development leaving an operculum scar. In the remaining species the outer
operculum is retained until just before flowering. Thus have no operculum scar.
The **anthers** are mostly oblong and versatile but in the Boxes, Ironbarks and several
species of the Divided-cotyledon group they are globular and adnate.

SINGLE-CAPPED EUCALYPTS (SUBGENUS MONOCALYPTUS) page 93
The buds have one **operculum**. Thus they have no operculum scar.
The **anthers** are reniform and versatile.

CHAPTER 2 DIVISION OF EUCALYPTS

Division of the Eucalypts of south-east Australia.
  1 **Buds scarred at junction of opercula and hypanthia**.
      2 **Bloodwood**
         E. tessellaris (Carbeen) (page 29): small to medium sized tree, found Woodenbong and north from Narrabri, New South Wales.
         Bark tessellated on lower trunk.
         Adult Leaves concolourous, narrow-lanceolate; venation transverse.
         Inflorescences axillary, compound.
         Fruit ovoid, thin walled; discs depressed.
         or
         E. eximia (Yellow Bloodwood) (page 28): small to medium sized tree, found north, south and west of Sydney.
         Bark yellow, papery, tessellated.
         Adult leaves concolourous, lanceolate; venation transverse.
         Inflorescences terminal, compound.
         Fruit large, ovoid to urceolate; discs depressed.

      2 **Not Bloodwood**. NSW VIC SA TAS
         Double-capped Eucalypts (page 31)

  1 **Buds scarred at tip of opercula**. Note - As an apical scar is easily missed exclude these species from the non-scarred group.
      2 **E. baileyana (Bailey's Stringybark) (page 30)**: medium sized tree, found coastal hills, north from Coffs Harbour, New South Wales.
         Bark stringybark.
         Adult leaves discolourous; venation transverse.
         Fruit large, globular to weakly urceolate; discs depressed; rim thin, undulate.

      2 **E. sturgissiana (Ettrema Mallee) (page 60)**: mallee, found Morton Nation Park, New South Wales.
         Matures partially with opposite, sessile **Juvenile leaves.**
         Fruit medium sized, hemispherical; discs flat; valves flat.

      2 **E. benthamii (Nepean River Gum) (page 65)**: medium to tall tree, found lower Nepean River, New South wales.
         Bark gum.
         Juvenile leaves opposite, sessile, broad-lanceolate to ovate, grey-green to glaucous.
         Fruit small, cupular to campanulate; discs flat to raised; valves exsert.

      2 **E. denticulata (page 69)**: tall tree, found on the Errinundra Plateau, Victoria, just crossing into New South Wales.
         Bark gum.
         Juvenile leaves opposite, sessile, broad-lanceolate to ovate, blue-green to glaucous, on square stems.
         Adult leaves denticulate.
         Fruit medium sized, cupular; discs depressed.

  1 continued on next page.

1 **Buds scarred; outer opercula shed in thin scales**.

    2 **E. desquamata (Devil's Peak Box) (page 83)**: mallee, found Devil's Peak, near Quorn, South Australia.
    Bark gum, coppery.
    Fruit medium sized, cupular; discs depressed.

1 **Buds not scarred, crossed at the apex of opercula**. Note - as the cross is easily missed exclude this species from the non-scarred group.
    2 **Sepalled Eucalypt**
    E. microcorys (Tallowwood) (page 30): medium to tall tree, found coast and nearby ranges, north from Cooranbong, New South Wales.
    Bark red-brown, spongy.
    Adult leaves glossy, discolourous.
    Fruit medium sized, conical to pyriform; discs weakly depressed.

1 **Buds not scarred**.
    2 **Bloodwood (page 27)** NSW VIC
    Bark bloodwood or gum.
    Adult leaves transverse venation.
    Inflorescences mainly terminal, compound.
    Fruit ovoid to urceolate; discs depressed.

    2 **Non-scarred Ironbark (page 77)** NSW VIC SA
    Bark ironbark or gum.
    Inflorescences axillary, simple.
    Buds in threes if gum, in threes or sevens if ironbark.
    Fruit hemispherical, cupular or cylindrical; discs depressed; rims thick.

    2 **Non-scarred box (page 76)** NSW VIC SA
    Tree or mallee.
    Bark box, on trunk or higher.
    Inflorescences terminal, compound.
    or
    Tree or mallee.
    Bark box, on trunk or higher.
    Inflorescences axillary, simple.
    Fruit cupular to ovoid; discs depressed.
    or
    Mallee.
    Bark gum.
    Inflorescences axillary, simple.
    Buds double conical, ovoid or fusiform.
    Fruit cupular to ovoid; discs depressed.

    2 **None of the above**.
    Single-capped Eucalypt (page 93) NSW VIC SA TAS

CHAPTER 3 BLOODWOODS

The **Bloodwoods** are identified in the first step of the key. As they have such characteristic fruit and bark, their identification usually offers little difficulty.

Division of the Bloodwoods.
1 **Buds** not scarred.
    2 **Bark** bloodwood.
    Red Bloodwood (page 27) NSW VIC

    2 **Bark** gum.
    Spotted Gum (page 29) NSW VIC

1 **Buds** scarred.
    2 **Bark** bloodwood, on the lower part of the trunk.
    Paper-fruited Bloodwood (page 29) NSW

    2 **Bark** yellow, papery, tessellated.
    Yellow Bloodwood (page 28) NSW

RED BLOODWOODS

Group characteristics
Medium sized trees.
Bark bloodwood.
Juvenile leaves opposite, becoming alternate, shortly petiolate; early ones rough.
    Adult leaves venation transverse.
    Inflorescences terminal, compound.
    Buds non-scarred, in sevens, pedicellate, ovoid; opercula hemispherical, weakly beaked.
    Fruit ovoid to urceolate; discs depressed.

Division of the Red Bloodwoods into Species
1 **Fruit** large, to 2 cm long, strongly urceolate.
    2 **Adult leaves** lanceolate, discolourous, dull or glossy, green.
    E. gummifera (Red Bloodwood): found on sandy soil, coast and nearby hills; New South Wales, far eastern Victoria. Q
    Juvenile leaves lanceolate to broad-lanceolate, peltate.
    Seeds not winged.

1 **Fruit** large to 2 cm long, weakly urceolate, white speckled.
    2 **Adult leaves** lanceolate, discolourous, glossy, green.
    E. intermedia (Pink Bloodwood): found coast and nearby hills, north from Gloucester, New South Wales. Q
    Juvenile leaves ovate, peltate.
    Seeds winged.

1 continued on next page.

1 **Fruit** very large, to 2.5 cm long, weakly urceolate.

2 **Adult leaves** narrow-lanceolate to lanceolate, discolourous, dull, grey-green.
E. dolichocarpa (Long-fruited Bloodwood): found western slopes, north from Narrabri, New South Wales. Q
Juvenile leaves broad-lanceolate.
Seeds winged.

2 **Adult leaves** lanceolate to broad-lanceolate, concolourous, dull, green to yellow-green.
E. opaca: found north-west from Darling River, New South Wales. Q NT
Juvenile leaves broad-lanceolate.
Seeds winged.

1 **Fruit** medium sized, to 1 cm long, strongly urceolate.

2 **Adult leaves** narrow-lanceolate, discolourous, glossy, green to grey-green.
E. trachyphloia (White Bloodwood): found western slopes, north from Goulburn River, New South Wales. Q
Juvenile leaves ovate, peltate.
Seeds not winged.

YELLOW BLOODWOOD

E. eximia (Yellow Bloodwood): small to medium sized tree, found on sandstone soils north, south and west of Sydney.
Bark yellow, papery, tessellated.
Juvenile leaves alternate, petiolate, broad-lanceolate to ovate, dull, grey-green.
Adult leaves lanceolate, concolourous, dull, green, prominent mid ribs; venation transverse.

Inflorescences terminal, compound.
Buds scarred, in sevens, sessile to shortly pedicellate, clavate; opercula slightly beaked.
Fruit large, to 2 cm long, ovoid to urceolate; discs depressed.
Seeds not winged.

CHAPTER 3 BLOODWOODS

SPOTTED GUMS

Group characteristics
Medium to tall forest trees.
Bark gum, characteristic mottled appearance.
Juvenile leaves alternate, shortly petiolate, ovate, glossy, green, early ones rough, sometimes peltate.
Adult leaves lanceolate, concolourous, semi-glossy, green; venation transverse.

Inflorescences axillary, some terminal, compound, pedunculate.
Buds non-scarred, some times scarred just before flowering, in threes, or sevens, pedicellate, ovoid; opercula hemispherical, weakly beaked.
Fruit ovoid to slightly urceolate; discs depressed.
Seeds not winged.

Division of the Spotted Gums into species
1 **Fruit** large, to 1.5 cm long.
    2 **Adult leaves** to 20 cm long.
      E. maculata (Spotted Gum): found on sandy soil, coast and nearby hills New South Wales; one isolated occurrence, eastern Victoria. Q

1 **Fruit** very large, to 2 cm long.
    2 **Adult leaves** to 30 cm long.
      E. henryi (Large-leaved Spotted Gum): found on stony shallow soil, coast and nearby hills, north from Grafton, New South Wales. Q

PAPER-FRUITED BLOODWOOD

E. tessellaris (Carbeen or Moreton Bay Ash): small to medium sized tree, found mainly on sandy soil, Woodenbong and north from Narrabri, New South Wales. Q
Bark tessellated, on lower trunk.
Juvenile leaves alternate, sessile to shortly petiolate, linear to narrow-lanceolate, glossy, green, early ones rough.
Adult Leaves narrow-lanceolate, green to grey-green, dull, concolourous; venation transverse.

Inflorescences axillary, compound.
Buds scarred, in threes, some sevens, pedicellate, clavate.
Fruit medium to large, to 1.1 cm long, ovoid to slightly urceolate, thin walled, weakly ribbed, discs depressed.

CHAPTER 4 SEPALLED EUCALYPT

The **Sepalled Eucalypts** are identified in the first step of the key. They show some evidence of sepal formation. As they have characteristic fruit, adult leaves and bark they usually offer little difficulty in identification.

E. baileyana (Bailey's Stringybark): medium sized forest tree, found on sandy soil, north from Coffs Harbour, New South Wales. Q
Bark stringybark.
Juvenile leaves opposite becoming alternate, shortly petiolate, broad-lanceolate to ovate, glossy, green, rough.
Adult leaves lanceolate, glossy, green, discolourous; venation transverse.

Inflorescences axillary, simple, pedunculate.
Buds scarred at apex, in sevens, pedicellate, clavate; opercula weakly beaked.
Fruit large, to 1.5 cm long, spherical to urceolate; discs depressed; rims thin, undulate.

E. microcorys (Tallowwood): medium to tall tree, found in wet forests, coast and nearby ranges, north from Cooranbong, New South Wales. Q
Bark red-brown, spongy.
Juvenile leaves alternate, petiolate, ovate, glossy, green.
Adult leaves lanceolate, glossy, green, discolourous; venation transverse.

Inflorescences axillary, some terminal, simple, some compound, pedunculate.
Buds non-scarred, in sevens or more, pedicellate, clavate; opercula crossed (partial sepal formation).
Fruit medium sized, to 0.9 cm long, conical to pyriform; discs weakly depressed; valves weakly exsert.

CHAPTER 5 DOUBLE-CAPPED EUCALYPTS

The **Double-capped Eucalypts** are the scarred Eucalypts after the exclusion of the scarred Bloodwoods and the inclusion of the non-scarred Boxes and the non-scarred Ironbarks.

The Double-capped Eucalypts can be divided into groups.

The **Transverse-veins (Section Transversaria) (page 35)** have discolourous adult leaves with transverse venation.

The **Divided-cotyledons (Section Bisectaria) (page 40)** have bisected cotyledons, ie. the first two leaves are divided into four. This cannot be used in the field. All but one species. E squamosa (Scaly Bark) are found in the mallee region. In this area they are identified by exclusion of all other species.

The **Ribbed-mallees (Section Dumaria) (page 43)** have ribbed buds, all are found in the mallee region and their young branches show oil glands in the pith. The only other species in South-east Australia with oil glands in the pith is E. trivalvis (Victoria Springs Mallee), a Divided-cotyledon.

The **Red Gums (Section Exsertaria) (page 46)** have globular or hemispherical fruit with strongly exsert valves, alternate, petiolate juvenile leaves, in most species gum bark and long opercula.

The **Oily-barks (Section Maidenaria) (page 51)** have oil glands in the bark. In several species it is strong enough to be smelt when crushed. They often have the buds in threes or the juvenile leaves opposite and sessile. The buds are all scarred, but three species, E. sturgissiana, E. denticulata and E. benthamii have the scar at the apex of the opercula.

The **Boxes and Ironbarks (Section Adnataria) (page 76)** have box, ironbark or gum bark. They often have terminal and compound inflorescences and usually have cupular to ovoid fruit. In near to half of the species the buds are scarred, while in the rest they are non-scarred until just before flowering.

Division of the scarred Double-capped Eucalypts
1 **Inflorescences** mainly terminal, compound.
            4 **Bark** ironbark.
            Ironbark (page 77) NSW

            4 **Bark** box or gum.
            Box (page 76) NSW VIC SA

1 **Inflorescences** axillary, compound.
            4 **Bark** gum.
               5 **Fruit** small, to 0.5 cm wide, cupular; discs flat; valves flat.
               E.michaeliana (Brittle Gum) (page 50) NSW

1 continued on next page.

1 **Inflorescences** axillary, frequently paired.

4 **Bark** grey, firm, flaky, tessellated.

5 **Fruit** medium sized, to 0.8 cm wide, hemispherical, slightly warty; rims wide; discs flat; valves exsert.
E. squamosa (Scaly Bark) (page 40) NSW

1 **Inflorescences** axillary, simple; **Buds** mainly in threes or less.

4 **Bark** box, on trunk or higher.

5 **Fruit** large, to 1.6 cm wide, cupular, cylindrical to campanulate; discs depressed.
E. longifolia (Woollybutt) (page 39) NSW

5 **Fruit** medium sized to 0.9 cm wide, globular; discs raised; valves exsert.
E. morrisii (Grey Mallee) (page 50) NSW

4 **Bark** matt, gum.

5 **Fruit** extra large, to 2 cm long, cupular; discs depressed; rims wide.
E. cosmophylla (Cup Mallee) (page 39) SA

4 **Bark** any other type.

5 **Fruit** large, hemispherical; discs flat, wide; valves strongly exsert.
E. scias (Large-fruited Red Mahogany)
(page 37) NSW

5 **Fruit** not as above.

6 **Buds** ribbed.
Ribbed-mallee (page 43) NSW VIC SA
Confirm by the presence of oil glands in the pith of young branches.

6 **Buds** not ribbed.
Oily-bark (page 51) NSW VIC SA TAS

1 **Inflorescences** axillary, simple; **Buds** in sevens or more.

2 Maturing with alternate, petiolate, discolourous **leaves.**

4 **Bark** box.

5 **Fruit** medium sized, to 0.8 cm wide, hemispherical; discs slightly raised; valves exsert.
E. angophoroides (Apple-topped Box) (page 65) NSW
VIC

2　　and　4 continued on next page.

4 **Bark** not box.

    5 **Fruit** medium sized, to 0.7 cm wide, conical; discs flat; valves slightly exsert.
       E. brookeriana (Brooker's Gum) (page 56) VIC TAS

    5 **Fruit** large, to 1.5 cm long, ovoid, ribbed, discs depressed.
       E. cladocalyx (Sugar Gum) (page 39) SA

    5 **Fruit** not as above.
       Transverse-vein (page 35) NSW VIC

2 Maturing with alternate, petiolate, concolourous **Adult leaves**; or opposite, sessile **Juvenile leaves**.
  3 Not Mallee region.
    4 **Bark** rough, mid trunk or higher.

      6 **Buds**; opercula >1.5 times longer than hypanthia.
        8 **Valves** exsert, needle-like.
         E. bakeri (Baker's Mallee) (page 40) NSW

        8 **Valves** exsert, not needle-like.
         E. exserta (Queensland Peppermint) (page 50) NSW

      6 **Buds**; opercula <1.5 times longer than hypanthia.
       Oily-bark (page 51) NSW VIC TAS

    4 **Bark** gum or rough basal.
      5 **Fruit**; valves strongly exsert.
        6 **Buds**; opercula <1.5 times longer than hypanthia.
         7 **Juvenile leaves** opposite, sessile.
         Oily-bark (page 51) NSW VIC TAS

        7 **Juvenile leaves** alternate, petiolate.
         Red Gum (page 46) NSW

      6 **Buds**; opercula >1.5 times longer than hypanthia.
       Red Gum (page 46) NSW VIC

    5 **Fruit**; valves flat to weakly exsert.
       Oily-bark (page 51) NSW VIC TAS

3 continued on next page.

3 Mallee region.

5 **Fruit** hemispherical to globular; valves exsert, not long needle like.
   6 **Buds**; opercula <1.5 times longer than hypanthia.
      7 **Juvenile leaves** opposite, sessile.
      Oily-bark (page 51) NSW VIC SA

      7 **Juvenile leaves** alternate, petiolate.
      Red Gum (page 46) NSW

   6 **Buds**; opercula >1.5 times longer than hypanthia.
   Red Gum (page 46) NSW VIC SA

5 **Fruit** conical; discs flat; valves flat or weakly exsert.
   E. ovata (Swamp Gum) (page 56) NSW VIC SA

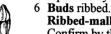

5 **Fruit** cupular to cylindrical; valves flat or exsert, not long needle like.
   6 **Buds** ribbed.
   Ribbed-mallee (page 43) NSW VIC SA
   Confirm by the presence of oil glands in the pith of young
   branches.

   6 **Buds** not ribbed; hypanthia cylindrical.
   E. goniocalyx (Long-leafed Box) (page 66) NSW VIC SA

   6 **Buds** not ribbed; ovoid to fusiform; opercula equal width to
   hypanthia.
      8 **Adult leaves** linear to narrow-lanceolate.
         9 **Bark** gum.
         E. leptophylla (Narrow-leaved Red
         Mallee) (page 40) NSW VIC SA

         9 **Bark** compact to large branches.
         E. cneorifolia (Kangaroo Island
         Narrow-leaved Mallee) (page 40) SA

      8 **Adult leaves** lanceolate.
      E. trivalvis (Victoria Springs Mallee) (page 40)
            SA

   6 **Buds** not ribbed; ovoid to fusiform or square in cross section
   (four angles); hypanthia wider than the opercula.
   Broad-flowered Mallee (page 42) NSW VIC SA

5 **Fruit** globular, cupular, cylindrical or urceolate; valves long, needle-
like.
Red Mallee (page 41) NSW VIC SA

CHAPTER 5 DOUBLE-CAPPED EUCALYPTS

TRANSVERSE-VEINS

Division of the Transverse-veins
1 **Bark** matt, gum.
   Grey gum (page 38) NSW

1 **Bark** gum or basal rough.
   Eastern Blue Gum (page 35) NSW

1 **Bark** rough to large branches or higher.
2 **Fruit** hemispherical; discs flat, valves exsert.

   Red Mahogany (page 36) NSW

2 **Fruit** cylindrical; discs depressed.
   Eastern blue gum (page 35) NSW VIC

Eastern Blue Gums

Group characteristics
Juvenile leaves alternate, petiolate, glossy, green.
Adult leaves green, strongly discolourous; venation transverse.
Inflorescences axillary, simple, pedunculate.
Buds scarred, in sevens or more; opercula beaked.

Division of the Eastern Blue Gums into species
1 **Juvenile leaves** found at maturity, ovate to orbicular.
2 **Adult leaves** lanceolate to broad-lanceolate, dull, rarely formed.
2 **Fruit** small, to 0.6 cm long, cylindrical to campanulate; discs flat; valves weakly exsert.
4 **Opercula** > 0.4 cm long

E. deanei (Mountain Blue Gum): tall to very tall forest tree, found coastal ranges, central New South Wales.
Bark gum, or basal rough.
Buds pedicellate, clavate.

4 **Opercula** < 0.4 cm long.
E. brunnea: tall forest tree, found northern tableland, north from Tyringham, New South Wales. Q
Bark gum, or basal rough.
Buds pedicellate, clavate.

1 continued on next page.

1 **Juvenile leaves** not found at maturity, ovate.
  2 **Adult leaves** lanceolate, glossy.
    3 **Fruit** medium sized, to 0.8 cm long, sub-glaucous, conical; discs depressed; valves exsert, in-curved.

E. grandis (Flooded Gum): tall to very tall tree, found near rain forests, coast and nearby ranges, north from Newcastle, New South Wales. Q
Bark gum, or basal rough.
Buds subsessile, ovoid, subglaucous.

  2 **Adult leaves** broad-lanceolate, glossy.
    3 **Fruit** medium sized, to 0.8 cm long, conical to pyriform; discs depressed; valves exsert, out-curved.

E. saligna (Sydney Blue Gum): medium to tall forest tree, found coast and nearby ranges New South Wales. Q
Bark gum, some basal rough.
Buds sub-sessile, ovoid to fusiform.
Grades into E. botryoides on south coast.

    3 **Fruit** large, to 1.2 cm long, cylindrical; discs depressed.

E. botryoides (Southern Mahogany or Bangalay): small to tall forest tree, found on sandy flats; central and southern coast New South Wales, east coast Victoria.
Bark mahogany to large branches.
Buds sub-sessile, clavate.

    3 **Fruit** large, to 1.8 cm long, cylindrical; discs depressed; valves flat, meet to form crosses.

E. robusta (Swamp Mahogany): small to medium sized forest tree, found on swampy coastal areas, north from Moruya, New South Wales. Q
Bark spongy, tessellated.
Buds pedicellate; opercula long beak.

Red Mahoganies

Group characteristics
Bark mahogany, sometimes tending stringybark.
Juvenile leaves alternate, petiolate, broad-lanceolate to ovate, glossy, green.
Adult leaves discolourous, glossy, green; venation transverse.
Inflorescences axillary, simple, pedunculate.
Buds scarred; hypanthia conical.
Fruit hemispherical; discs flat, wide; valves strongly exsert.

Division of the Red Mahoganies into species

1 **Fruit** large >1 cm wide.

E. scias (Large-fruited Red Mahogany)

Adult leaves lanceolate to broad-lanceolate.

2 **Buds** in sevens or threes, pedicellate; opercula conical or hemispherical, beaked.
ssp. scias: small to tall forest tree, found Cessnock to Sydney, New South Wales.
Fruit to 2 cm wide.

2 **Buds** in sevens or threes, sessile; opercula hemispherical.
ssp. apoda: small tree, found east of Tenterfield, New South Wales.
Fruit to 1.6 cm wide.

2 **Buds** in sevens or threes, pedicellate; opercula hemispherical, beaked.
ssp. callimastha: small to tall forest tree, found southern coast and nearby hills, Helensburgh to Bateman's Bay, New South Wales.
Fruit to 1.4 cm wide.

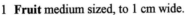

1 **Fruit** medium sized, to 1 cm wide.

2 **Buds** in sevens, sub-sessile; opercula conical.
E. notabilis (Mountain Mahogany): small to medium sized tree, found on plateaux, Blue Mountains, near Armidale and Gibraltar Range National Park, New South Wales. Q
Adult leaves lanceolate.

2 **Buds** in sevens, pedicellate; opercula high conical to horned.
E. resinifera (Red Mahogany): medium to tall forest tree.
Adult leaves lanceolate.

3 **Opercula** <3 times longer than hypanthia.
ssp. resinifera: found central coast and nearby hills, Taree to Huskisson, New South Wales.

3 **Opercula** >3 times longer than hypanthia.
ssp. hemilampra: found northern coast and nearby hills, north from Kempsey, New South Wales. Q

CHAPTER 5 DOUBLE-CAPPED EUCALYPTS

Grey Gums

Group characteristics
Bark matt, gum, irregular patches, orange to grey.
Juvenile leaves alternate, petiolate, narrow-lanceolate to broad-lanceolate, glossy, green.
Adult leaves lanceolate, glossy, green, discolourous, venation transverse.
Inflorescences axillary, some terminal, simple, some compound, pedunculate.
Buds scarred, occasionally some non-scarred, in sevens, pedicellate.
Fruit; discs flat, wide; valves strongly exsert.

Division of the Grey Gums into species
1 **Opercula** hemispherical to weakly conical.
    2 **Fruit** small, to 0.6 cm wide; hypanthia hemispherical to conical.
      E. propinqua (Small Fruited Grey Gum): medium to tall forest tree, found northern and central coast and nearby ranges, north from Wyong, New South Wales. Q

1 **Inner opercula** conical, narrower than hypanthia;
  wrinkled **outer opercula** often retained.
    2 **Fruit** medium sized, to 0.9 cm wide; hypanthia hemispherical.
      E. biturbinata (Grey Gum): medium sized forest tree, found northern coast and nearby ranges, north from Gloucester, New South Wales. Q

    2 **Fruit** large, to 1.5 cm wide; hypanthia hemispherical to conical
      E. canaliculata (Large-fruited Grey Gum): medium to tall tree, found from Dungog to Gloucester region, New South Wales.

1 **Opercula** conical.
    2 **Fruit** medium sized, to 1 cm wide; hypanthia hemispherical to cylindrical.
      E. punctata (Grey Gum): medium sized tree, found central coast and nearby ranges, Liverpool Ranges to Nowra, New South Wales.

CHAPTER 5 DOUBLE-CAPPED EUCALYPTS

Concolourous-leaved Transverse-veins

E. longifolia (Woollybutt): medium to tall forest tree, found on heavy soils, central and southern coast New South Wales.

Bark box, to large branches.
Juvenile leaves alternate, petiolate, ovate to broad-lanceolate, dull, grey-green.
Adult leaves narrow-lanceolate to lanceolate, falcate, dull, grey-grey, concolourous; venation transverse.
Inflorescences axillary, simple; peduncles long curved.
Buds scarred, in threes, double conical to fusiform; pedicels long.
Fruit large, to 1.6 cm wide, cupular, cylindrical to campanulate; discs depressed; valves flat or weakly exsert.

E. cosmophylla (Cup Gum): mallee to small tree, found Kangaroo Island and southern Lofty Ranges, South Australia.

Bark matt, gum.
Juvenile leaves opposite then alternate, petiolate, ovate to orbicular, dull, grey-green.
Adult leaves lanceolate to broad-lanceolate, dull, grey-green, concolourous.
Inflorescences axillary, simple; peduncles short.
Buds scarred, in threes, sub-sessile, ovoid.
Fruit large, to 2 cm long, cupular; discs depressed; rims thick.

E. cladocalyx (Sugar Gum): small to tall tree, found Kangaroo Island, southern Eyre Peninsula and Mount Remarkable, South Australia.
Bark matt, gum, yellow, grey, blue patches.
Juvenile leaves alternate, petiolate, orbicular, glossy, green.

Adult leaves lanceolate, glossy, dark green, discolourous; venation transverse.
Inflorescences, axillary, some terminal, simple, some compound, pedunculate.
Buds scarred, in sevens or more, pedicellate, cylindrical, ribbed; opercula low hemispherical, pointed.
Fruit large, to 1.5 cm long, ovoid, ribbed; discs depressed.

DIVIDED-COTYLEDONS

E. squamosa (Scaly Bark): small tree, found north and south of Sydney.
Bark grey, firm, flaky, tessellated.
Juvenile leaves alternate, shortly petiolate, broad-lanceolate to ovate, dull, grey-green.
Adult leaves lanceolate, dull, grey-green, concolourous.

Inflorescences axillary, frequently paired, pedunculate.
Buds scarred, in sevens or more, pedicellate, ovoid, slightly warty.
Fruit small to medium sized, to 0.8 cm wide, hemispherical, slightly warty; discs flat; valves exsert.

E. cneorifolia (Kangaroo Island Narrow-leaved Mallee): mallee, found Kangaroo Island and southern tip, Fleurieu Peninsula, South Australia.
Bark compact, to large branches.
Juvenile leaves sub-opposite, sub-sessile, narrow-lanceolate, erect, green.
Adult leaves linear to narrow-lanceolate, erect, glossy, green, concolourous.

Inflorescences axillary, simple, pedunculate.
Buds scarred, in sevens or more, sessile, ovoid.
Fruit medium sized, to 0.8 cm wide, hemispherical; discs flat; valves weakly exsert.

E. leptophylla (Narrow-leaved Red Mallee): mallee, found widespread in dry country, mallee areas; New South Wales, Victoria, South Australia. WA
Bark gum.
Juvenile leaves opposite, sessile, ovate, glaucous.
Adult leaves narrow-lanceolate, erect, glossy, green, concolourous; stems red, warty.

Inflorescences axillary, simple, pedunculate.
Buds scarred, in sevens or more, pedicellate, fusiform; opercula conical, often red.
Fruit small, to 0.5 cm wide, globular; discs flat; valves exsert.

E. trivalvis (Victoria Springs Mallee): mallee, found south of Lake Gairdner, South Australia. NT WA
Bark rough, on trunk, grey to coppery gum above.
Juvenile leaves alternate, petiolate, lanceolate to ovate, green.

Adult leaves lanceolate to ovate, dull, green, grey or glaucous, concolourous; young branches have oil glands in pith.
Inflorescences axillary, simple, pedunculate.
Buds scarred, in sevens, pedicellate, ovoid.
Fruit medium sized, to 0.9 cm long, cylindrical; discs depressed; valves three, flat.

E. bakeri: mallee to small tree, found Yetman and Warialda, New South Wales. Q
Bark rough, on trunk, gum above.
Juvenile leaves alternate, petiolate, linear to narrow-lanceolate, glossy, green.

Adult leaves narrow-lanceolate, glossy, green, concolourous.
Inflorescences axillary, simple, pedunculate.
Buds scarred, in sevens or more, pedicellate, fusiform; opercula horned.
Fruit small, to 0.5 cm wide cupular; discs flat; valves exsert, long.

CHAPTER 5 DOUBLE-CAPPED EUCALYPTS

Red Mallees

Group characteristics
Mallees, may be small trees.
Adult leaves concolourous.
Inflorescences axillary, simple, pedunculate.
Buds scarred, in sevens or more, pedicellate.
Fruit; discs depressed; valves exsert, long needle-like.

Division of the Red Mallees into species
1 **Bark** gum or basal compact to box.
    2 **Buds** ovoid; opercula narrower than the hypanthia, conical or hemispherical.
        3 **Adult leaves** narrow-lanceolate to lanceolate, glossy, green.
        E. oleosa (Giant or Glossy-leaved Red Mallee): found widespread on dry flats, mallee areas; New South Wales, Victoria, South Australia. WA
        Juvenile leaves opposite to spiral, sessile, linear, dull, green to grey-green.
        Fruit small, to 0.6 cm long, cupular to globular.

    2 **Buds** ribbed; hypanthia cylindrical, constricted in middle; opercula hemispherical, long beak.
        3 **Adult leaves** lanceolate, glossy, green.
        E. flocktoniae (Merrit): found Eyre Peninsula, South Australia. WA
        Juvenile leaves opposite, sessile, ovate to broad-lanceolate, glaucous.
        Fruit medium sized, to 1 cm long, urceolate, ribbed.

    2 **Buds**; hypanthia hemispherical; opercula hemispherical, strongly beaked.
        3 **Adult leaves** lanceolate to broad-lanceolate, dull, grey-green; petioles to 2 cm long.
        E. socialis (Red Mallee): found widespread on sand dunes, mallee areas; New South Wales, Victoria, South Australia. NT WA
        Juvenile leaves opposite then alternate, sessile, ovate, dull, grey-green.
        Fruit medium sized, to 0.8 cm long, globular.

        3 **Adult leaves** rarely formed; matures with opposite, sessile, ovate to orbicular, glaucous **juvenile leaves**.
        E. gillii (Curly Mallee): found north of Broken Hill, New South Wales; northern Flinders Ranges, South Australia.
        Adult leaves if formed opposite to subopposite, broad-lanceolate, dull, grey-green to glaucous.
        Buds glaucous.
        Fruit medium sized, to 0.8 cm long, globular, glaucous.

1   and   3   continued on next page.

3 **Adult leaves** lanceolate to broad-lanceolate, glossy or dull, green; petioles >2 cm long.
E. yumbarrana (Yumbarra Mallee): found on sand dunes, west Eyre Peninsula, South Australia.
Juvenile leaves opposite, sessile, broad-lanceolate to ovate, green.
Fruit medium to large, to 1.2 cm long, globular to weakly urceolate.

1 **Bark** box, to large branches.
  2 **Buds** pedicellate, fusiform.
    3 **Adult leaves** lanceolate, dull, grey-green.
E. yalatensis (Yalata Mallee): found western Eyre Peninsula, South Australia. WA
Juvenile leaves sub-opposite, sessile, ovate, green.
Fruit small, to 0.5 cm long, pear shaped.

Broad-flowered Mallees

Group characteristics
Mallees, may be small trees.
Bark gum, or compact to box at base.
Juvenile leaves opposite to alternate, petiolate, lanceolate, glaucous.
Adult leaves narrow-lanceolate to lanceolate, glossy, green, concolourous.
Inflorescences axillary, simple, pedunculate.
Buds scarred, in sevens; opercula narrower than hypanthia; staminodes present.

Division of the Broad-flowered Mallees into species
1 **Buds** clavate; opercula hemispherical.
  2 **Fruit** small to medium sized, to 0.7 cm long, cupular to cylindrical; discs depressed; rims thin.
E. gracilis (Yorrell or White Mallee): found widespread in dry country, mallee areas; New South Wales, Victoria, South Australia. WA

1 **Buds** cylindrical, square in cross section (four angles).
  2 **Fruit** large, to 1.5 cm long, barrel to urceolate, square in cross section; discs depressed
E. calycogona (Square-fruited Mallee)
    3 **Buds** weakly squared.

ssp calycogona (Square-fruited Mallee): found in dry country, mallee areas; Victoria, South Australia, and into New South Wales. WA

    3 **Buds** strongly squared.
ssp spaffordii (Square-fruited Mallee): found central Eyre Peninsular, South Australia.

CHAPTER 5 DOUBLE-CAPPED EUCALYPTS

RIBBED-MALLEES

Group characteristics
Mallees, may be small trees.
Juvenile leaves alternate, petiolate.
Adult leaves concolourous.
Young branches have oil globules in pith.
Inflorescences axillary, simple, pedunculate.
Buds scarred, ovoid, faintly to strongly ribbed.
Fruit cupular to cylindrical, faintly to strongly ribbed; discs depressed; rims thick.

Division of the Ribbed-mallees into species
1 **Buds** pedicellate, in sevens or more; opercula conical to slightly beaked, ribbed, about equal width to hypanthia.
    2 **Bark** gum or basal compact to box.
        3 **Adult leaves** lanceolate, glossy, grey-green to green; young stems squared.

          E. calcareana (Nundroo Mallee): usually tree, found in Western Eyre Peninsula, South Australia. WA
          Juvenile leaves ovate, glaucous to dull, green.
          Fruit medium sized, to 1 cm long.

        3 **Adult leaves** lanceolate, dull, grey-green.

          E. dumosa (White Mallee): found widespread in dry country, mallee areas; New South Wales, Victoria, South Australia.
          Juvenile leaves ovate, dull, grey-green.
          Fruit medium sized, to 0.9 cm long.

        3 **Adult leaves** broad-lanceolate, dull, grey-grey to glaucous.
          5 **Buds** and **fruit** green to yellow-green.
             E. cyanophylla (Blue-leaved Mallee): found at the junction of the three states; New South Wales, Victoria, South Australia.
             Juvenile leaves ovate, dull, grey-green.
             Fruit medium sized, to 1 cm long.

          5 **Buds, fruit** and **small branches** glaucous.
             E. cretata (Darke Peak Mallee): found near Darke Peak, Eyre Peninsula, South Australia.
             Juvenile leaves ovate, dull, grey to grey-green.
             Fruit medium sized, to 0.8 cm long.

1 continued on next page.

1 **Buds** shortly pedicellate, in sevens; opercula hemispherical to weakly beaked, strongly ribbed, wider than hypanthia.

   2 **Bark** gum or basal compact to box.

      3 **Adult leaves** lanceolate, glossy, green.

         E. pileata (Capped Mallee): mallee to small tree, found Eyre Peninsula, South Australia. WA
         Juvenile leaves ovate, glaucous to dull, green.
         Fruit medium sized, to 1 cm long.

      3 **Adult leaves** lanceolate, dull, green to grey-green.

         E. percostata: found in isolated spots, Flinders Ranges, South Australia.
         Juvenile leaves ovate, dull, grey-green.
         Fruit medium sized, to 0.8 cm long.

1 **Buds** sub-sessile, in sevens; opercula conical to beaked, weakly ribbed, equal width to hypanthia; bases tapered; peduncles 1 cm long.

   2 **Bark** gum or basal compact to box.

      3 **Adult leaves** lanceolate, glossy, green.

         E. anceps (Kangaroo Island Mallee): found eastern Kangaroo Island and southern South Australia, and into western Victoria. WA
         Juvenile leaves ovate, green.
         Peduncles 1 cm long.
         Fruit medium sized, to 0.8 cm long.

1 **Buds** sessile, in sevens; opercula conical to weakly beaked, ribbed, equal width to hypanthia; bases square; peduncles 0.5 cm long.

   2 **Bark** gum or basal compact to box.

      3 **Adult leaves** lanceolate, glossy, green, leathery.

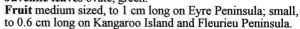

         E. conglobata (Port Lincoln Mallee): found Kangaroo Island and tips Fleurieu, York and Eyre Peninsulas, South Australia. WA
         Juvenile leaves ovate, green.

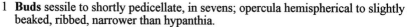

         Fruit medium sized, to 1 cm long on Eyre Peninsula; small, to 0.6 cm long on Kangaroo Island and Fleurieu Peninsula.

1 **Buds** sessile to shortly pedicellate, in sevens; opercula hemispherical to slightly beaked, ribbed, narrower than hypanthia.

   2 **Bark** gum or basal compact to box.

      3 **Adult leaves** lanceolate to broad-lanceolate, glossy, grey-green, leathery.

         4 **Fruit** medium, to large to 1.5 cm long; valves exsert.
         E. rugosa (Kingscote Mallee): found Kangaroo Island and southern coast, South Australia.
         Juvenile leaves ovate, green.

1 continued on next page.

1 **Buds** pedicellate, in sevens; opercula hemispherical to slightly beaked, faintly ribbed, narrower than hypanthia.
    2 **Bark** box, to large branches.
        3 **Adult leaves** narrow-lanceolate, glossy, green.

            4 **Fruit** medium sized, to 0.8 cm long, valves exsert.
            E. brachycalyx (Gilja): found about St. Vincent's Gulf, South Australia. WA
            Juvenile leaves ovate, green.

1 **Buds** pedicellate, in threes or sevens; opercula hemispherical, flat topped, ribbed, equal width or wider than hypanthia.
    2 **Bark** gum or basal compact to box.
        3 **Adult leaves** narrow-lanceolate, glossy, green.

            4 **Fruit** small to medium sized, to 1 cm long, valves exsert.
            E. concinna (Victoria Desert Mallee): found western Eyre peninsula, South Australia. WA
            Juvenile leaves lanceolate, green.

1 **Buds** pedicellate, in threes or sevens; opercula hemispherical, strongly beaked ribbed, equal width to hypanthia.
    2 **Bark** gum or basal compact to box.
        3 **Adult leaves** lanceolate to broad-lanceolate, leathery, glossy, green.

            4 **Fruit** large, to 1.3 cm long.
            E. costata (Ridge-fruited Mallee): found on sand dunes, mallee areas; New South Wales, Victoria, South Australia.
            Juvenile leaves ovate, dull, grey-green to green, leathery.

            4 **Fruit** very large, to 2 cm long.
            E. angulosa (Ridge-fruited Mallee): found Kangaroo Island, Fleurieu Peninsula and tip of Eyre Peninsula, South Australia. WA
            Juvenile leaves ovate, dull, grey-green to green, leathery.

CHAPTER 5 DOUBLE-CAPPED EUCALYPTS

RED GUMS

Group characteristics
Bark gum, patches of different grey, often basal plates.
Juvenile leaves alternate, petiolate.
Adult leaves concolourous.
Inflorescences axillary, simple, pedunculate.
Buds scarred, in sevens or more.
Fruit; valves strongly exsert.

Division of the Red Gums into species
1 **Fruit** cupular; discs raised, separated by groove from valves.
    2 **Buds** pedicellate, fusiform, green; opercula conical.
        3 **Juvenile leaves** ovate, dull, green.
        E. pumila (Pokolbin Mallee): mallee, found only Broken Back
Range, Pokolbin, New South Wales.
Adult leaves lanceolate, glossy, green.
Fruit medium sized, 0.9 cm wide.

    2 **Buds** pedicellate, fusiform, green; opercula horned.
        3 **Juvenile leaves** broad-lanceolate, dull, grey-green.
        E. seeana (Narrow-leaved Red Gum): medium to tall tree,
found on poorly drained soil, northern coast New South Wales. Q
Adult leaves narrow-lanceolate, dull, green.
Fruit small to medium sized, to 0.7 cm wide.

    2 **Buds** pedicellate, cylindrical, green; opercula high conical.
        3 **Juvenile leaves** ovate to orbicular, dull, grey-green to glaucous.
        E. interstans: medium sized tree, found east of Tenterfield, New
South Wales. Q
Adult leaves lanceolate, dull, green.
Fruit small to medium sized, to 0.9 cm wide.

    2 **Buds** pedicellate, cylindrical, glaucous; opercula cylindrical, round ended.
        3 **Juvenile leaves** ovate to orbicular, glaucous.
        E. prava (Orange Gum): small tree, found on poor soil, New
England Tableland, New South Wales. Q
Bark often orange.
Adult leaves broad-lanceolate to ovate, dull, grey-green to glaucous.
Fruit medium sized, to 1 cm wide.

    2 **Buds** pedicellate, cylindrical, green; opercula cylindrical, round ended.
        3 **Juvenile leaves** ovate, dull, grey-green.
        E. bancroftii (Orange Gum): a small tree, found north coast, north
from Port Macquarie, New South Wales. Q
Bark often orange.
Adult leaves lanceolate to broad-lanceolate, dull, grey-green.
Fruit medium sized, to 0.9 cm wide.

1 continued on next page.

CHAPTER 5 DOUBLE-CAPPED EUCALYPTS

1 **Fruit** hemispherical, discs slightly raised, separated by groove from valves.
  2 **Buds** pedicellate, green, opercula conical to hemispherical.
    3 **Juvenile leaves** narrow-lanceolate to lanceolate, dull, green.

     E. parramattensis (Parramatta Red Gum): small tree.
     Adult leaves narrow-lanceolate to lanceolate, dull, green.
      4 **Fruit** small, < 0.7 cm wide.
       ssp parramattensis: found western Sydney area.

      4 **Fruit** medium sized, 0.7 to 0.9 cm wide.
       ssp decadens: found Hunter Valley, New South Wales.

1 **Fruit** globular; discs strongly raised, >45 degrees, continuous with valves.
  2 **Buds** fusiform, green; opercula horned.
    3 **Juvenile leaves** large, ovate to orbicular, dull, green.
     E. amplifolia (Cabbage Gum): medium to tall tree.
     Adult leaves lanceolate to broad-lanceolate, dull, green.
     Fruit small to medium sized, to 0.8 cm wide.

      5 **Buds** pedicellate.
       ssp. amplifolia: found central coast and nearby hills,
       Coffs Harbour to Bega, New South Wales.

      5 **Buds** sessile.
       ssp. sessiliflora found Stanthorpe to Armidale and
       Casino, New South Wales. Q

    3 **Juvenile leaves** broad-lanceolate to ovate, glossy, green.
      5 **Buds** pedicellate.
       E. tereticornis (Forest Red Gum): medium to tall forest
       tree, found coast and nearby hills; New South Wales,
       East Gippsland, Victoria. Q
       Adult leaves narrow-lanceolate to lanceolate, dull,
       green.
       Fruit medium sized, to 0.8 cm wide.
       E. camaldulensis (page 48) Dandenong and Traralgon
       form may key out as **E. tereticornis**.

  2 **Buds** pedicellate, green; opercula high conical.
    3 **Juvenile leaves** ovate to orbicular, dull, grey-green.
     E. blakelyi (Blakely's Red Gum): medium sized tree, found
     tablelands New South Wales, and into north-eastern Victoria.
     Adult leaves narrow-lanceolate to lanceolate, dull, green to grey-
     green.
     Fruit small to medium sized, to 0.7 cm wide.
     E. camaldulensis (page 48) Dandenong and Traralgon form may key
     out as **E. blakelyi**.

1 and 2 continued on next page.

2 **Buds** pedicellate, fusiform, glaucous; opercula high conical.
   3 **Juvenile leaves** ovate, glaucous.

      E. glaucina (Slaty Red Gum): small to medium sized tree, found Casino and Taree to Broke, New South Wales.
      Adult leaves lanceolate, dull, green to grey-green.
      Fruit medium sized, to 1 cm wide.

2 **Buds** pedicellate, green; opercula hemispherical, beaked.
  E. camaldulensis (River Red Gum): medium sized tree.
  Adult leaves narrow-lanceolate to lanceolate, dull, green to grey-green.
  Fruit small to medium sized, to 0.8 cm wide.
    3 **Juvenile leaves** narrow-lanceolate to lanceolate, blue-green to green.
      4 **Opercula** medium sized beak.

      ssp camaldulensis: found along river courses Murray-Darling Basin; New South Wales, Victoria, South Australia, and southern Victoria except East Gippsland. Q NT WA

    3 **Juvenile leaves** broad-lanceolate, grey-green.
      4 **Opercula** very small beak.

      ssp obtusa: found northern South Australia. Q NT WA

    3 **Juvenile leaves** broad-lanceolate to ovate, grey-green.
      4 **Opercula** very long beak.

      ssp subspecies: found near Dandenong and Traralgon, Victoria.

1 **Fruit** hemispherical; discs flat to slightly raised, < 45 degrees, continuous with valves.
  2 **Buds** pedicellate, ovoid, glaucous; opercula high conical.
    3 **Juvenile leaves** ovate to orbicular, glaucous.

    E. dealbata (Tumbledown Red Gum): small tree, found on rocky ridges, western part of tablelands, New South Wales, and into north-eastern Victoria. Q
    Adult leaves lanceolate, dull, grey-green to glaucous.
    Fruit small to medium sized, to 0.7 cm wide.

2 **Buds** pedicellate, ovoid, green; opercula high conical.
    3 **Juvenile leaves** ovate to orbicular, dull, green.
      4 **Fruit** small, to 0.6 cm wide.
        5 Small tree, found on sandy hollows, north from Gilgandra, New South Wales.
        E. chloroclada (Dirty Gum). Q
        Adult leaves lanceolate, dull, green.

2,   3   5   continued on next page.

5 Small tree found near Beechworth, Victoria.
E. species.
Adult leaves lanceolate, dull, green.

3 **Juvenile leaves** broad-lanceolate to ovate, dull, green to grey-green.
4 **Fruit** medium sized, to 0.8 cm wide.
E. vicina: mallee found from Cobar to Broken Hill to Ivanhoe, far western New South Wales.
Adult leaves narrow-lanceolate to lanceolate, dull, green.

3 **Juvenile leaves** narrow-lanceolate to lanceolate, dull, green to grey-green.
4 **Fruit** small to medium sized, to 0.7 cm wide.
E. dwyeri (Dwyer's Red Gum): mallee to small tree, found on rocky ridges, western parts of central tableland New South Wales. Q
Adult leaves narrow-lanceolate to lanceolate, dull, green.

4 **Fruit** small, to 0.5 cm wide.
E. nandewarica (Mallee Red Gum): mallee, found Mount Kaputar National Park, New South Wales.
Buds sometime in threes.
Adult leaves narrow-lanceolate, dull, green.

2 **Buds** sub-sessile, ovoid, green; opercula high hemispherical.
3 **Juvenile leaves** ovate to orbicular, dull, green.
E. flindersii (South Australian Grey Mallee): mallee or small tree, found Northern Flinders Ranges, South Australia.
Adult leaves narrow-lanceolate to lanceolate, dull, green to grey-green.
Fruit medium sized, to 0.9 cm wide.

Rough Barked Red Gum

E. morrisii (Grey Mallee): mallee to small tree, found Bourke to Cobar, western New South Wales.
Bark box, on trunk.
Juvenile leaves alternate, petiolate, linear to narrow-lanceolate, dull, green.
Adult leaves narrow-lanceolate to lanceolate, dull, grey-green, concolourous.

Inflorescences axillary, simple, pedunculate.
Buds scarred, mainly in threes, sessile to shortly pedicellate; hypanthia hemispherical; opercula high conical.
Fruit medium sized, to 0.9 cm wide, globular; discs raised; valves strongly exsert.

E. exserta (Queensland Peppermint): small tree found north from Ashford, New South Wales. Q
Bark peppermint, to large branches.
Juvenile leaves alternate, petiolate, linear, dull, green to grey-green.
Adult leaves narrow-lanceolate to lanceolate, semi-glossy, green, concolourous.

Inflorescences axillary, simple, pedunculate.
Buds scarred, in sevens, shortly pedicellate, ovoid to fusiform; opercula high conical.
Fruit medium sized, to 0.9 cm wide, globular; discs raised; valves strongly exsert.

Compound Inflorescence Gum

E. michaeliana (Brittle Gum): small to medium sized tree, found restricted to Hillgrove and Wyong areas, New South Wales. Q
Bark gum.
Juvenile leaves alternate, petiolate, lanceolate to broad-lanceolate, dull, green.
Adult leaves lanceolate, dull, grey-green, concolourous to faintly discolourous.

 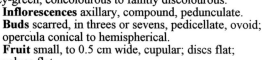

Inflorescences axillary, compound, pedunculate.
Buds scarred, in threes or sevens, pedicellate, ovoid; opercula conical to hemispherical.
Fruit small, to 0.5 cm wide, cupular; discs flat; valves flat.

CHAPTER 5 DOUBLE-CAPPED EUCALYPTS

OILY-BARKS

The **Oily-barks** can be artificially divided into groups.

Swamp Gums (page 56) have mainly broad-lanceolate to ovate adult leaves.

Black Peppermints (page 58) have narrow adult leaves and compact or latticed bark.

Tasmanian Yellow Gums (page 59) have crenulate, green juvenile leaves.

Individuals (page 60) are a group of unrelated, distinctive species.

Silver Gums (page 62) have mainly glaucous juvenile leaves.

Apple Boxes (page 65) have pedicellate buds and box bark.

Long-leaved Boxes (page 66) have sessile, cylindrical buds and box bark.

Grey Gums (page 67) have shortly pedicellate, cylindrical buds.

Blue Gums (page 68) have large, glaucous juvenile leaves on very square stems.

Scent-barks (page 70) have bark that smells of eucalyptus when crushed.

False Stringybarks (page 71) have stringybark like bark.

Brittle Gums (page 72) have very powdery gum bark.

Manna Gums and Others (page 73) have mainly lanceolate, green juvenile leaves.

Division of the Oily-barks
1 **Bark** stringybark, medium length fibres, on trunk or higher.
      3 **Juvenile leaves** opposite, sessile, orbicular, glaucous.

        4 **Buds** in threes.
            6 **Fruit** medium sized, conical; discs weakly raised; valves weakly exsert..
            False Stringybark (page 71) NSW VIC

            6 **Fruit** large, globular; discs raised; valves exsert.
            E. chapmaniana (Bogong Gum) (page 62)
                    NSW VIC

        4 **Buds** in sevens.
            6 **Fruit** medium sized, conical; discs weakly raised; valves weakly exsert.
            False Stringybark (page 71) NSW VIC

1 continued on next page.

1 **Bark** box, on trunk or higher.

    4 **Buds** in threes.

        6 **Fruit** medium sized, campanulate; discs raised; valves exsert.
        E. kartzoffiana (Araluen Gum) (page 62) NSW

    4 **Buds** in sevens.

      5 **Buds** sessile, ovoid to fusiform or hypanthia cylindrical; opercula conical.

        6 **Fruit** medium sized, cylindrical to cupular.
        Long-leaved Box (page 66) NSW VIC SA

        6 **Fruit** medium sized, conical; valves exsert.
        E. quadrangulata (White-topped Box) (page 69) NSW

      5 **Buds** pedicellate, ovoid to double conical.

        6 **Fruit** medium sized; hypanthia hemispherical; discs slightly raised; valves exsert.
        Apple Box (page 65) NSW VIC

      5 **Buds** pedicellate; hypanthia cylindrical.

        6 **Fruit** medium sized, cylindrical to cupular; valves flat or exsert.
        Grey Gum (page 67) NSW VIC

1 **Bark** rough, to large branches, not stringybark or box, deep layers smelling of eucalyptus when crushed.

    4 **Buds** in sevens.

        6 **Fruit** small, hemispherical; discs raised.
        Scent bark (page 70) NSW VIC

1 **Bark** rough, on trunk or higher, not stringybark or box, not smelling of eucalyptus.

    4 **Buds** in threes.

        6 **Fruit** medium sized, globular; disc raised; valves exsert.
        Manna Gum and others (page 73)
                    NSW VIC SA TAS

    4 **Buds** in sevens or more.

        7 **Leaves at maturity** partially or fully, opposite, sessile.
        Individual (page 60) VIC

1   and   7 continued on next page.

7 **Leaves at matures** alternate, petiolate,
broad-lanceolate to ovate.
Swamp Gum (page 56)
NSW VIC SA TAS

7 **Leaves at mature** alternate, petiolate
narrow-lanceolate to lanceolate.
　　8 **Bark** extends to small branches.
　　Black Peppermint (page 58)
　　NSW VIC TAS

　　8 **Bark** not to small branches.
　　Manna Gum and others (page 73)
　　NSW VIC

1 **Bark** gum or basal rough
　2 **Leaves at maturity** partially or fully, opposite, sessile.
　　3 **Juvenile leaves** green.
　　　4 **Buds** single.
　　　E. vernicosa (Varnished Gum) (page 59) TAS

　　　4 **Buds** in threes.
　　　E. recurva (page 61) NSW VIC TAS

　　　4 **Buds** in sevens.
　　　Individual (page 60) NSW VIC

　　3 **Juvenile leaves** glaucous.
　　　4 **Buds** in threes.
　　　Silver Gum (page 62) NSW VIC TAS

　　　4 **Buds** in sevens.
　　　Individual (page 60) NSW VIC

　2 **Leaves at maturity** alternate, petiolate.
　　3 **Juvenile leaves** opposite, sessile, broad-lanceolate to narrower, green.
　　　4 **Buds** in threes or sevens.
　　　Manna Gum and others (page 73) NSW VIC SA TAS

　　3 **Juvenile leaves** opposite, sessile, broad-lanceolate to ovate, glossy to
　　semi-glossy, green; stems round or weakly squared.
　　　4 **Buds** in threes.

　　　　6 **Fruit** medium to large, cupular, valves exsert.
　　　　Tasmanian Yellow Gum (page 59) TAS

　　　　6 **Fruit** medium sized, hemispherical to globular;
　　　　discs weakly raised; valves exsert.
　　　　E. imlayensis (Mount Imlay Mallee) (page 61)
　　　　NSW

3 and 4 continued on next page.

53

4 **Buds** in sevens.

6 **Fruit** medium sized, hemispherical; discs flat; valves flat.
E. kitsoniana (Gippsland Mallee or Bog Mallee) (page 61) VIC

6 **Fruit** medium sized, cupular to cylindrical; discs depressed.
Grey Gum (page 67) NSW VIC

6 **Fruit** medium sized, conical; discs flat; valves flat to weakly exsert.
Swamp Gum (page 56) NSW VIC SA

3 **Juvenile leaves** opposite, sessile, ovate to orbicular, dull, green, grey-green or blue-green; stems round or weakly squared.

4 **Buds** in threes.

6 **Fruit** medium sized, hemispherical to globular; discs raised; valves exsert.
E. dalrympleana (Mountain Gum) (page 75) NSW VIC TAS

6 **Fruit** medium to large, cupular or urceolate.
Silver Gum (page 62) TAS

4 **Buds** in sevens.

6 **Fruit** medium sized, hemispherical; discs flat; valves exsert.
E. dunnii (Dunn's White Gum) (page 65) NSW

6 **Fruit** medium sized, hypanthia campanulate; discs weakly raised; valves exsert.
E. dalrympleana (Mountain Gum) (page 75) NSW

3 **Juvenile leaves** opposite, sessile, large, broad-lanceolate to ovate, glaucous; stems very squared.

6 **Fruit** large to very large, conical to campanulate; discs wide; valves weakly exsert.
Blue Gum (page 68) NSW

6 **Fruit** medium sized, medium sized, globular; discs raised; valves exsert.
E. rubida (Candlebark) (page 75) NSW

3 continued on next page.

3 **Juvenile leaves** opposite, sessile, broad-lanceolate to orbicular, glaucous; stems round or weakly squared.

    4 **Buds** in threes.

        6 **Fruit** medium sized, medium sized, globular; discs raised; valves exsert.
        E. rubida (Candlebark) (page 75) NSW

        6 **Fruit** medium sized, hemispherical to globular; discs raised; valves flat to weakly exsert.
        E. elaeophoia (Brumby Gum) (page 61) VIC

        6 **Fruit** cup, cylindrical, campanulate or urceolate; discs depressed.
        Silver Gum (page 62) NSW VIC TAS

    4 **Buds** in sevens.

        6 **Fruit** medium sized, medium sized, globular; discs raised; valves exsert.
        E. rubida (Candlebark) (page 75) NSW

        6 **Fruit** small to medium sized, hemispherical; discs raised; valves weakly exsert.
        Brittle Gum (page 72) NSW

        6 **Fruit** small, cupular to campanulate; valves exsert.
        White Gum (page 65) NSW

3 **Juvenile leaves** alternate, petiolate, lanceolate, grey-green to glaucous; stems round.

    4 **Buds** in sevens.

        6 **Fruit** medium sized, conical; discs flat; valves weakly exsert.
        E. cadens. (page 57) VIC

        6 **Fruit** small to medium sized, hemispherical; discs raised; valves weakly exsert.
        E. mannifera (Brittle Gum) (page 72) NSW

3 **Juvenile leaves** alternate, petiolate, broad-lanceolate to ovate, green; stems round.
Swamp Gum (page 56) NSW VIC SA

CHAPTER 5 DOUBLE-CAPPED EUCALYPTS

Swamp Gums

Group characteristics
Adult leaves green.
Juvenile leaves alternate, some early ones opposite, petiolate.
Inflorescences axillary, simple, pedunculate.
Buds scarred, in sevens, pedicellate.

Division of the Swamp Gums into species
1 **Buds** ovoid.

   2 **Fruit** small, to 0.5 cm wide, hemispherical; discs flat; valves weakly exsert.

     3 **Bark** compact, to large branches.

       4 **Adult leaves** broad-lanceolate, undulate, concolourous, glossy.
         E. yarraensis (Yarra Gum): small to medium sized tree, found only in several isolated spots across southern Victoria.
         Juvenile leaves ovate, dull, green.

1 **Buds** double conical.

   2 **Fruit** medium sized, to 0.7 cm wide (large, to 1.3 cm wide in South-east of South Australia extending just into Victoria), conical; discs flat; valves flat to weakly exsert.

     3 **Bark** gum, untidy plates for variable distance up trunk.

       4 **Adult leaves** broad-lanceolate to ovate, concolourous, glossy, few oil glands, new growth green.

         5 **Juvenile leaves** ovate, dull, green.
           E. ovata (Swamp Gum): small to medium sized tree, found widely in poorly drained areas; southern tableland New South Wales, across southern Victoria, Lofty Ranges, Kangaroo Island and south-east, South Australia, north and east Tasmania.

     3 **Bark** gum, tessellated on lower trunk.

       4 **Adult leaves** lanceolate to broad-lanceolate, concolourous or discolourous, glossy, many oil glands, new growth green.

         5 **Juvenile leaves** opposite then alternate, shortly petiolate, ovate, sub-glossy, green, crenulate.
           E. brookeriana (Brooker's Gum): medium to tall forest tree, found Tasmania, King Island, Otway National Park and isolated spots central Victoria.

     3 **Bark** gum, basal rough on young trees only.

       4 **Adult leaves** lanceolate to broad-lanceolate, concolourous, glossy, green, many oil glands, new growth often glaucous.

         6 **Juvenile leaves** opposite, then alternate, petiolate, lanceolate to ovate, sub-glossy, green, sub-crenulate.
           E. strzeleckii: medium sized tree found on hills, south and west Gippsland, Victoria.

1 and 2 continued on next page.

2 **Fruit** small to medium sized, to 0.8 cm wide, conical; discs flat; valves exsert.

    3 **Bark** gum, often some basal plates.

        4 **Adult leaves** ovate, round ended, concolourous, dull, green or glaucous; petioles < 1 cm long.

        E. aquatica (Mountain Swamp Gum or Broad-leaved Sally): mallee, found Paddy's River, New South Wales.
Juvenile leaves ovate, glossy, green.
Fruit medium sized, to 0.7 cm wide.

        4 **Adult leaves** ovate, round ended, concolourous, dull, green or glaucous; petioles > 1 cm long.
E. camphora (Mountain Swamp Gum or Broad-leaved Sally)

        Juvenile leaves ovate, glossy, green.

            5 **Petioles** < 2 cm long.
ssp. camphora: mallee to small tree, found west of Blue Mountains, New South Wales.
Fruit small, to 0.5 cm wide.

            5 **Petioles** > 2 cm long.

                6 **Adult leaves** > 2.5 cm wide.
ssp. humeana: mallee to small tree, found on poorly drained mountain areas; southern tablelands New South Wales, and north-east Victoria.
Fruit small, to 0.6 cm wide.

                6 **Adult leaves** < 2.5 cm wide.
ssp. relicta: mallee found north-east of Guyra, New South Wales. Q
Fruit medium sized, to 0.8 cm wide.

        4 **Adult leaves** lanceolate, concolourous, new growth glaucous.
E. cadens (Wangaratta Gum): straggly small tree, found Warby Range near Wangaratta, Victoria.
Juvenile leaves lanceolate, glaucous.
Fruit medium sized, to 0.7 cm wide.

1 **Buds**; hypanthia conical to cylindrical; opercula conical, weakly beaked.

    2 **Fruit** medium sized, to 0.9 cm long, cupular; discs depressed; rims thick.

        3 **Bark** gum, some basal plates.

            4 **Adult leaves** lanceolate, concolourous.
E. barberi (Barber's Gum): mallee or small tree, found in isolated spots on low hills, east coast Tasmanian.
Juvenile leaves broad-lanceolate, green; young stems red, warty.

CHAPTER 5 DOUBLE-CAPPED EUCALYPTS

Black Peppermints

Group Characteristics
Small to medium sized trees.
Adult leaves concolourous.

Inflorescences axillary, simple, pedunculate.
Buds scarred, in sevens, pedicellate, ovoid.
Fruit small, to 0.5 cm wide, hemispherical; discs flat.

Division of the Black Peppermints into species
1 **Bark** compact.
    2 **Juvenile leaves** opposite to alternate, shortly petiolate, broad-lanceolate to ovate, dull, green.
        3 **Adult leaves** narrow-lanceolate to lanceolate, glossy, green.
           4 **Peduncles** <0.5 cm long.
               5 **fruit** crowded (tending sessile); valves weakly exsert.
E. aggregata (Black Gum): found in central and southern tablelands New South Wales, Woodend, Victoria.

           4 **Peduncles** >0.5 cm long.
               5 **Fruit** not crowded (pedicellate); valves weakly exsert.
E. rodwayi (Swamp Peppermint): found in swampy areas, central plateau Tasmania.
Juvenile leaves nearly sessile.

1 **Bark** fibrous, coarsely latticed (compact on young trees).
    2 **Juvenile leaves** crowded, alternate, subsessile, linear to narrow-lanceolate, dull, grey-green.
        3 **Adult leaves** linear to narrow-lanceolate, dull, grey-green.
               5 **Fruit**; valves exsert.
E. nicholii (Narrow-leaved Black Peppermint): found from Niangala to Glen Innes, New South Wales.

    2 **Juvenile leaves** alternate, petiolate, ovate, crenulate, dull, green.
        3 **Adult leaves** lanceolate, dull, green, grey-green.
               5 **Fruit**; valves flat to weakly exsert.
E. acaciiformis (Wattle-leaved Peppermint): found in isolated areas, New England Tableland, New South Wales.

Tasmanian Yellow Gums

Group characteristics
Bark gum.
Juvenile leaves opposite to subopposite, sessile to subsessile, ovate, crenulate, glossy, green.
Adult leaves concolourous.
Inflorescences axillary, simple.
Buds scarred, ovoid; opercula slightly beaked.
Fruit hemispherical; discs depressed; rims thick; valves weakly exsert to exsert.

Division of the Tasmanian Yellow Gums into species
1 **Leaves at maturity** juvenile, opposite, sessile small, to 2.5 cm long, ovate,
    2 **Inflorescences** shortly pedunculate.
        3 **Buds** single, sessile.
            4 **Fruit** medium sized, to 0.8 cm wide.

                E. vernicosa (Varnished Gum): stunted shrubs, found only above tree line on mountain tops, south-western Tasmania.

1 **Leaves at maturity** adult, broad-lanceolate, sub-crenulate, leathery, glossy, green.
    2 **Inflorescences** pedunculate.
        3 **Buds** in threes, sessile to shortly pedicellate.
            4 **Fruit** medium sized, to 0.8 cm wide.

                E. subcrenulata (Tasmanian Alpine Yellow Gum): small tree, found on mountains, southern Tasmania.
                Bark pink, grey, yellow patches.

            4 **Fruit** large, to 1.3 cm wide, angular.

                E. johnstonii (Tasmanian Yellow Gum): tall to very tall tree, found mountains, southern Tasmania.
                Bark pink, grey, yellow patches.

CHAPTER 5 DOUBLE-CAPPED EUCALYPTS

Individuals

Group characteristics
Juvenile leaves opposite, sessile.
Adult leaves, if formed, concolourous.
Inflorescences axillary, simple, pedunculate.

Division of the Individuals into species
1 **Leaves at maturity** fully or partially opposite, sessile.
    2 **Juvenile leaves** small, broad-lanceolate to ovate, glossy, green.
        3 **Buds** scarred, in sevens, sessile, ovoid.
        E. parvula (Small-leaved Gum): small tree, found near Kybean, New South Wales.
        Bark gum.
        Adult leaves when formed, sub-opposite, lanceolate, dull, green.
        Fuit small, to 0.4 cm wide, cupular; discs weakly raised; valves flat.

    2 **Juvenile leaves** ovate, cordate, crenulate, glaucous
        3 **Buds** scarred, in sevens or more, pedicellate, glaucous; opercula hemispherical, beaked.
        E. crenulata (Victorian Silver Gum or Buxton Gum): small tree, found only in two isolated spots near Buxton and Yering, Victoria.
        Bark compact on trunk.
        Fruit small, to 0.4 cm wide, cupular, glaucous; discs depressed.

    2 **Juvenile leaves** ovate to orbicular, grey-green to glaucous.
        3 **Buds** scarred at apex, in sevens, sessile, ovoid, glaucous.
        E. sturgissiana (Ettrema Mallee): mallee, found in Morton National Park, New South Wales.
        Bark gum.
        Adult leaves lanceolate, glossy, grey-green to glaucous.
        Fruit medium sized, to 0.7 cm wide, hemispherical, glaucous; discs flat; valves flat.

    2 **Juvenile leaves** ovate, glaucous.
        3 **Buds** scarred, in sevens, sessile, ovoid, glaucous; outer opercula retained as brown cap.
        E. neglecta (Omeo Gum): small tree, found near streams in sub-alpine regions Victoria.
        Bark compact, on lower half of trunk.
        Adult leaves lanceolate, green.
        Fruit small, to 0.6 cm wide, hemispherical to conical; discs flat; valves flat to weakly exsert.

1 continued on next page.

CHAPTER 5 DOUBLE-CAPPED EUCALYPTS

1 **Leaves at maturity** mainly alternate, petiolate.
    2 **Juvenile leaves,** ovate, green, leathery.
        3 **Buds** scarred, in sevens, sessile, ovoid, green.
        E. kitsoniana (Bog Mallee): mallee to small tree, found Victorian

        coast.
        Bark gum.
        Adult leaves broad-lanceolate, green, leathery.
        Fruit medium sized, to 0.8 cm wide, hemispherical; discs flat; valves
        flat.

Green-barks

Group characteristics
Mallee to small tree.
Bark gum, green when first exposed.
Juvenile leaves opposite, sessile, ovate.
Adult leaves lanceolate, glossy to semi-glossy, green, concolourous.
Inflorescences axillary, simple, pedunculate.
Buds scarred, in threes, sessile, ovoid.
Fruit medium sized, to 0.8 cm wide, globular; hypanthia hemispherical; discs raised.

Division of the Green-barks
1 **Fruit;** valves exsert.
    2 **Juvenile leaves** glossy, dark green.
        E. imlayensis (Mount Imlay Mallee): found Mount Imlay, southern
        New South Wales.

1 **Fruit;** valves flat to weakly exsert.
    2 **Juvenile leaves** glaucous.
        E. elaeophloia (Brumby Gum): found Brumby Ridge, near Mount
        Nunniong, north-eastern Victoria.

E. recurva: mallee, found near Braidwood, New South Wales.
Bark gum.
Juvenile leaves found at maturity, opposite, sessile, very small, to 3 cm long, ovate,
glossy, green.

        Inflorescences axillary, simple, pedunculate.
        Buds scarred, in threes, subsessile, ovoid; outer opercula splitting
        into four, remaining as brown lumps on scar.
        Fruit small, to 0.5 cm wide, cupular; discs raised; valves flat.

Silver Gums

Group characteristics
Juvenile leaves opposite, sessile.
Adult leaves concolourous, petiolate.
Inflorescences axillary, simple, pedunculate.
Buds scarred, in threes.

Division of the Silver Gums into species

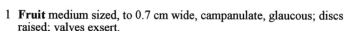

1 **Fruit** large, to 1.1 cm wide, glaucous; hypanthia cylindrical to campanulate; discs raised; valves exsert.
    2 **Juvenile leaves** orbicular, glaucous.
        E. chapmaniana (Bogong Gum): medium sized forest tree, found on high mountains, north-eastern Victorian, and just into New South Wales.
        Bark stringybark, on trunk.
        Adult leaves alternate, lanceolate, dull, grey-green.
        Buds sub-sessile, double conical, glaucous.

1 **Fruit** medium sized, to 0.7 cm wide, campanulate, glaucous; discs raised; valves exsert.
    2 **Juvenile leaves** ovate, glaucous.
        E. kartzoffiana (Araluen Gum): medium sized tree, found Araluen, New South Wales.
        Bark box, on the trunk.
        Adult leaves alternate, narrow-lanceolate, dull, green to grey-green.
        Buds sessile, glaucous; hypanthia cylindrical; opercula conical.

1 **Fruit** large, to 1.4 cm wide, campanulate, glaucous; discs raised; valves weakly exsert.
    2 **Juvenile leaves** ovate to orbicular, cordate, glaucous.
        E. saxatilis (Suggan Buggan Mallee): mallee to small tree, found Mount Wheeler and several nearby sites, north-eastern Victoria.
        Bark gum.
        Adult leaves alternate, lanceolate, dull, grey-green.
        Buds sessile, clavate; hypanthia cylindrical; opercula flat, beaked, wider than hypanthia.
        Fruit glaucous.

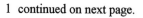

1 continued on next page.

1 **Fruit** large, to 1.3 cm long, cupular, glaucous; discs depressed; rims thick.

    2 **Juvenile leaves** orbicular, crenulate, cordate, glaucous, found at maturity.
    E. cordata (Silver Gum): small tree found in several isolated spots, southern Tasmania.
    Bark gum.
    Adult leaves alternate, lanceolate, dull, grey-green or glaucous, rarely formed.
    Buds sessile, glaucous; hypanthia cylindrical; opercula flat, beaked.

    2 **Juvenile leaves** opposite, sessile, ovate to orbicular, cordate, glaucous.
    E. glaucescens (Tingiringi Gum): mallee or small (rarely tall) tree, found on high mountains; south-eastern New South Wales, eastern Victoria.
    Bark gum to basal box.
    Adult leaves alternate, lanceolate to broad-lanceolate, dull, grey-green.
    Buds sessile, glaucous; hypanthia cylindrical; hypanthia conical; opercula beaked.

1 **Fruit** medium sized, <1 cm long, cupular.

    2 **Juvenile leaves** orbicular, cordate, glaucous, found at maturity.
    E. pulverulenta (Silver-leaved Gum): mallee to small straggly tree, found Blue Mountains and near Bredbo, New South Wales.
    Bark gum, bronze, glaucous.
    Adult leaves sub-opposite, lanceolate, glaucous, rarely formed.
    Buds sessile, ovoid, glaucous; opercula low conical, beaked.
    Fruit to 0.9 cm long, glaucous; discs flat; valves flat to exsert.

    2 **Juvenile leaves** orbicular, connate, glaucous, partially found at maturity.
    E. perriniana (Spinning Gum): mallee to small tree, found on high mountains; south-eastern New South Wales, eastern Victoria, south-eastern Tasmania.
    Bark gum, bronze, some basal rough.
    Adult leaves subopposite, lanceolate, dull, grey-green to glaucous.
    Buds sub-sessile, ovoid, glaucous; operculum hemispherical.
    Fruit to 0.7 cm long, glaucous; discs flat or depressed; valves flat.

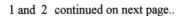

1 and 2 continued on next page..

2 **Juvenile leaves** orbicular, crenulate, cordate, glaucous.
E. morrisbyi (Morrisby's Gum): small to medium sized tree, found in two isolated spots, Risdon and Cremorne, Tasmania.
Bark gum, glaucous small branches.
Adult leaves alternate, lanceolate, dull, grey-green to glaucous.
Buds pedicellate, glaucous; hypanthia conical; opercula flat, beaked.
Fruit to 0.9 cm long, glaucous; discs depressed; rims thin.

2 **Juvenile leaves** ovate, dull, grey-green.
E. archeri (Alpine Cider Gum): mallee to small tree, found at high altitude, north-central and north-eastern Tasmania.
Bark gum.
Adult leaves alternate, lanceolate, dull, grey-green.
Buds sessile, ovoid, opercula hemispherical, beaked.
Fruit to 0.8 cm long; discs depressed.

1 **Fruit** medium sized, to 0.9 cm long, cylindrical to slightly urceolate, usually glaucous; discs depressed.

    2 **Juvenile leaves** ovate to orbicular, crenulate, dull, grey-green.
E. gunnii (Cider Gum): small to medium sized tree, found central tablelands, Tasmania.
Bark gum, green to pink-grey, some basal rough.
Adult leaves ovate to broad-lanceolate, dull, grey-green.
Buds sub-sessile, clavate, glaucous; opercula hemispherical, beaked.

1 **Fruit** large, to 1.6 cm long, urceolate, often glaucous; discs depressed.
    2 **Juvenile leaves** orbicular, glaucous at high altitudes, glossy, green at low altitudes.

E. urnigera (Urn Gum): small to tall tree, found southern Tasmania.
Bark gum.
Adult leaves lanceolate to broad-lanceolate, dull, green or subglaucous.
Buds glaucous, hypanthia cylindrical, constricted in middle; opercula flat, beaked; pedicels long.

CHAPTER 5 DOUBLE-CAPPED EUCALYPTS

White Gums

Group characteristics
Medium to tall trees.
Bark gum, some basal rough.
Juvenile leaves opposite, sessile, broad-lanceolate to ovate, dull, grey-green to glaucous.
Adult leaves concolourous, lanceolate, dull, green.
Inflorescences axillary, simple, pedunculate.
Buds in sevens, sub-sessile, ovoid.
Fruit small, to 0.5 cm wide, cupular to campanulate; discs flat to raised; valves exsert.

Division of the White Gums into species
1 **Scar** at apex of opercula.

   E. benthamii (Nepean River Gum): found lower Nepean River, New South Wales.

1 **Scar** at middle of bud.

   E. dorrigoensis (Dorrigo White Gum): found near Dorrigo, New South Wales.

Apple Boxes

Group characteristics
Juvenile leaves opposite to sub-opposite, sessile to sub-sessile, crenulate, ovate to orbicular, cordate, dull.
Adult leaves dull to semi-glossy, green.
Inflorescences axillary, simple, pedunculate.
Buds scarred, in sevens, pedicellate; opercula weakly beaked.
Fruit medium sized, to 0.8 cm wide, conical to hemispherical; discs weakly raised; valves exsert.

Division of the Apple Boxes into species
1 **Bark** box, on lower trunk, gum above.
   2 **Adult leaves** concolourous, narrow-lanceolate to lanceolate.
      3 **Juvenile leaves** grey-green.

         E. dunnii (Dunn's White Gum): medium to tall forest tree, found near Urbenville and Dorrigo, New South Wales. Q
         Buds ovoid, green.

1 The **bark** box, to all but small branches.
   2 **Adult leaves** discolourous, narrow-lanceolate to lanceolate.
      3 **Juvenile leaves** green.

         E. angophoroides (Apple-topped Box): medium to tall forest tree, found coast and nearby hills; south from Towrang, New South Wales, eastern Victoria.
         Buds ovoid, green.

   2 continued on next page.

65

2 **Adult leaves** concolourous, lanceolate.
   3 **Juvenile leaves** glaucous.

      4 **Buds** ovoid, green.
      E. bridgesiana (Apple Box): small to medium sized tree, found tablelands New South Wales, eastern and north-eastern Victoria. Q

      4 **Buds** double conical, glaucous.
      E. malacoxylon (Moonbi Apple Box): small to medium sized tree, found Inverell to Niangala, New South Wales.

Long-leaved Boxes

Group characteristics
Small to medium sized trees.
Bark box, to all but small branches.
Juvenile leaves opposite, sessile, orbicular.
Adult leaves lanceolate, concolourous.
Inflorescences axillary, simple, pedunculate.
Buds scarred, in sevens, sessile.

Division of the Long-leaved Boxes into species
1 **Buds** green; hypanthia cylindrical; opercula conical.
E. goniocalyx (Long-leafed Box): mallee to medium sized tree, found tablelands New South Wales; southern, central and western Victoria; Lofty and Flinders Ranges, South Australia.

      Juvenile leaves dull, grey-green.
      Adult leaves glossy, green.
      Fruit medium sized, to 1 cm long, cupular to cylindrical, discs flat to descending; valves flat to exsert.

1 **Buds** glaucous; hypanthia cylindrical, opercula conical.
E. nortonii (Mealy Bundy): small tree, found on poor sites; tableland, New South Wales, north-eastern Victoria.

      Juvenile leaves glaucous.
      Adult leaves dull, grey-green to glaucous.
      Fruit medium sized, to 1 cm long, cupular, ribbed, glaucous; discs depressed to flat; valves flat to exsert.

1 **Buds** ovoid, green.
E. banksii (Tenterfield Woollybutt): small to medium sized tree, found north from Armidale, New South Wales. Q
      Juvenile leaves cordate, dull, grey-green to glaucous.
      Adult leaves dull, grey-green.
      Peduncles short.
      Fruit medium sized, to 0.6 cm long, cupular ; discs flat; valves exsert.

Grey Gums

Group characteristics
Juvenile leaves opposite, sessile.
Adult leaves lanceolate, dull to semi-glossy, green, concolourous.
Inflorescences axillary, simple, pedunculate.
Buds scarred, in sevens, pedicellate; hypanthia cylindrical, angular; opercula conical

Division of the Grey Gums into species

1 **Fruit** medium sized, to 1 cm long, cupular to cylindrical; discs depressed; valves flat.
    2 **Juvenile leaves** broad-lanceolate to ovate, glossy, green; stems round or weakly squared.

      E. cypellocarpa (Mountain Grey Gum or Monkey Gum): small to very tall forest tree, found coast and nearby ranges; south from Tamworth, New South Wales, eastern Victoria.
      Bark gum, some basal plates.

    2 **Juvenile leaves** broad-lanceolate to ovate, glossy, green; stems very squared.
      E. alaticaulis: medium sized tree, found Grampians National Park and Otway Ranges, Victoria.
      Bark box, on trunk.
      The Grampian form has very glossy juvenile leaves.

    2 **Juvenile leaves** broad-lanceolate to ovate, glaucous; stems round or weakly squared.
      E. volcanica: medium sized tree, found Mount Kaputar and Warrumbungle National Parks, New South Wales.
      Bark box, on trunk.

1 **Fruit** medium sized, to 1 cm long, cupular to conical; discs flat; valves exsert.
    2 **Juvenile leaves** broad-lanceolate to ovate, glossy, green; stems round or weakly squared.
      E. retinens: small to medium sized tree, found tops of gorges, upper Macleay and Guy Rivers, northern New South Wales.
      Bark box to large branches.

CHAPTER 5 DOUBLE-CAPPED EUCALYPTS

Blue Gums

Group characteristics
Medium to tall forest trees.
Bark gum, some basal plates.
Juvenile leaves opposite, sessile, broad-lanceolate to ovate, cordate, dull, blue-green to glaucous; stems very square.
Intermediate leaves very long to 25 cm, lanceolate.
Adult leaves narrow-lanceolate to lanceolate, glossy, green, concolourous.
Inflorescences axillary, simple.

Division of the Blue Gums into species
1 **Buds** scarred between opercula and hypanthia; hypanthia conical, angular;
   opercula flat, beaked, wider than hypanthia.
>   2 **Fruit** conical to campanulate; discs wide, valves weakly exsert.
>   >   3 **Peduncle** present.

>   >   >   4 **Buds** in sevens, sessile to shortly pedicellate, weakly warty, weakly glaucous.
>   >   >   **E. maidenii (Maiden's Gum)**: found coastal ranges, south from Shoalhaven River, New South Wales, and just into eastern Victoria.
>   >   >   **Fruit** medium sized, to 1 cm wide, usually green.

>   >   >   4 **Buds** in threes, sub-sessile, warty, weakly glaucous.
>   >   >   **E. pseudoglobulus (Gippsland Blue Gum)**: found coast and nearby ranges, eastern Victoria, and into New South Wales, several isolated spots west of Melbourne.
>   >   >   **Fruit** large, to 1.5 cm wide, some glaucous.

>   >   3 **Peduncles** short or absent.
>   >   >   4 **Buds** in threes, sessile, warty, glaucous.
>   >   >   **E. bicostata (Southern Blue Gum or Eurabbie)**: found north-eastern Victoria, southern New South Wales tableland; with occurrences northern tablelands New South Wales, southern Victoria.
>   >   >   **Fruit** large, to 2 cm wide, glaucous.

1   and   4 continued on next page.

4 **Buds** in threes or single, sessile, warty, glaucous.

E. species (South Gippsland Blue Gum): found South Gippsland including Wilson's Promontory, Phillip Island; Otway Ranges Victoria; Bass Strait Islands. **Fruit** large when in threes, extra large when single, to 2.5 cm wide, glaucous.

4 **Buds** single, sessile, warty, glaucous.

E. globulus (Tasmanian Blue Gum): found eastern Tasmania. **Fruit** extra large, to 2.5 cm wide, glaucous.

1 **Buds** scarred between opercula and hypanthia, ovoid; hypanthia cylindrical; opercula conical.

  2 **Fruit** small to medium sized, to 0.7 cm long, cupular to cylindrical, shiny; discs depressed.

    4 **Buds** in sevens, sessile; **inflorescences** pedunculate.

     5 **Adult leaves** not denticulate.

E. nitens (Shining Gum): found New England, Barrington Tops National Parks, mountains of southern New South Wales, east of Melbourne to West Gippsland, Victoria.

1 **Buds** scarred at apex, fusiform to ovoid.

  2 **Fruit** medium sized, to 0.8 cm long, cylindrical; discs depressed.

    4 **Buds** in sevens, sessile; **inflorescences** pedunculate.

     5 **Adult leaves** denticulate.

E. denticulata (Errinundra Gum): found Errinundra Plateau, Victoria, and just into southern New South Wales.

The White-topped Box

E. quadrangulata (White-topped Box): tall forest tree, found eastern tablelands north from Bundanoon, New South Wales. Q

Bark box, trunk or to large branches.

Juvenile leaves opposite, sessile, broad-lanceolate to ovate, cordate, dull, green, on very, square stems.

Adult leaves narrow-lanceolate to lanceolate, denticulate, dull to semi-glossy, green, concolourous.

Inflorescences axillary, simple, pedunculate.

Buds scarred, in sevens, sessile, ovoid to fusiform.

Fruit medium sized, to 0.7 cm long, conical; discs flat; valves exsert.

CHAPTER 5 DOUBLE-CAPPED EUCALYPTS

Scent-barks

Group Characteristics
Small to medium sized trees.
Bark spongy, coarse longitudinal furrows; deep layers smelling of eucalyptus when crushed.
Juvenile leaves at first opposite then alternate.
Adult leaves narrow-lanceolate to lanceolate, green to grey-green, dull, concolourous.
Inflorescences axillary, simple, pedunculate.
Buds scarred, in sevens, shortly pedicellate, ovoid.
Fruit small, to 0.6 cm wide, hemispherical to campanulate; discs raised; valves exsert.

Division of the Scent Barks into species
There are still further species to be described in this group.
1 **Adult leaves** narrow-lanceolate, glossy, green to grey-green.
   2 **Juvenile leaves** sessile, linear, glossy, green.
   E. species (Scent-bark): found from western Grampians to Little Desert, Victoria.

   2 **Juvenile leaves** sessile, lanceolate, glossy, green.
   E. species (Scent-bark): found south-western Victoria.

1 **Adult leaves** narrow-lanceolate to lanceolate, dull, grey-green.
   2 **Juvenile leaves** at first sessile, then petiolate, narrow-lanceolate, dull, green.
   E. corticosa (Scent-bark): found only localised area near Rylstone, New South Wales.

   2 **Juvenile leaves** sessile, then petiolate, broad lanceolate, dull, grey-green.
   E. ignorabilis (Scent-bark): found southern coast New South Wales, Walhalla and eastern Victoria.

   2 **Juvenile leaves** at first sessile, then alternate, linear to narrow-lanceolate, falcate, glaucous.
   E. species (Scent-bark): found north-central Victoria.

1 **Adult leaves** narrow-lanceolate to lanceolate, semi-glossy, green.
   2 **Juvenile leaves** at first sessile, then petiolate, broad-lanceolate, dull, green.
   E. species (Scent-bark): found Gippsland and east of Melbourne.

   2 **Juvenile leaves** sessile, ovate, glaucous.
   E. aromaphloia (Scent-bark): found from Mount William, Grampians National Park to Wombat State Forest, western Victoria.

CHAPTER 5 DOUBLE-CAPPED EUCALYPTS

False Stringybarks

Group characteristics
Small to medium sized trees.
Bark stringybark, to large branches, medium length fibres.
Juvenile leaves opposite, sessile, orbicular, cordate, glaucous.
Adult leaves concolourous.
Inflorescences axillary, simple, pedicellate.
Buds scarred, usually glaucous.
Fruit conical, often glaucous; discs weakly raised; valves weakly exsert.

Division of the False Stringybarks into species
1 **Fruit** small, to 0.5 cm wide.
    2 **Buds** in sevens, pedicellate, ovoid.
        3 **Leaves at maturity** mainly alternate, petiolate.

        E. nova-anglica (New England Peppermint): found north from
Nowendoc, New England Tableland, New South Wales. Q
Adult leaves alternate, petiolate, narrow-lanceolate to lanceolate, dull
to semi-glossy, grey-green.

    2 **Buds** in threes, sessile, double conical.
        3 **Leaves at maturity** mainly alternate, petiolate.
        E. species found Swanpool, Victoria.
        Adult leaves alternate, petiolate, lanceolate, dull, grey-green.

1 **Fruit** medium sized, 0.6 to 0.9 cm wide.
    2 **Buds** in sevens, sessile, double conical.
        3 **Leaves at maturity** mainly alternate, petiolate.
        E. cephalocarpa (Mealy Stringybark or Silver stringybark): found
eastern Melbourne.
        Adult leaves alternate, petiolate, lanceolate, dull, grey-green.

        3 **Leaves at maturity** mainly opposite, sessile, orbicular or broad-
lanceolate.
        E. conspicua: found in swampy areas, East Gippsland, Victoria.
        Adult leaves opposite to sub-opposite, lanceolate to broad-lanceolate,
dull, grey-green to glaucous.

    2 **Buds** in threes, sessile, double conical.
        3 **Leaves at maturity** mainly opposite, sessile, orbicular.

        E. cinerea (Argyle Apple): found Sofala to
Tumut, southern tableland, New South Wales.
Adult leaves opposite to sub-opposite, lanceolate
to broad-lanceolate, dull, grey-green to glaucous.

    3 continued on next page.

3 **Leaves at maturity** opposite or alternate, ovate or lanceolate.

    4 Rocky out crop, Namadgi National Park, south of Canberra.
E. triplex
Adult leaves opposite to sub-opposite, lanceolate to broad-lanceolate, dull, grey-green to glaucous.

    4 Beechworth or Big River, Victoria.
E. alligatrix
Adult leaves alternate, petiolate, broad-lanceolate, glaucous at Beechworth, lanceolate, grey-green at Big River.

Brittle Gums

Group Characteristics
Small trees.
Bark gum, powdery, red, grey or white patches.
Adult leaves dull, green to grey-green, concolourous.
Inflorescences axillary, simple, pedunculate.
Buds scarred, in sevens, ovoid.
Fruit hemispherical; discs raised; valves weakly exsert.

Division of the Brittle Gums into species
1 **Juvenile leaves** alternate to sub-opposite, shortly petiolate, linear to narrow-lanceolate, dull, blue-green to glaucous.

    2 **Adult leaves** narrow-lanceolate to lanceolate.

        3 **Fruit** small, to 0.7 cm long.

E. mannifera (Brittle Gum): found central and southern tableland, south from Rylstone, New South Wales, and eastern Victoria.
Buds sessile to pedicellate, green.

1 **Juvenile leaves** opposite to sub-opposite, subsessile, ovate, glaucous.

    2 **Adult leaves** lanceolate to broad-lanceolate.

        3 **Fruit** small, to 0.6 cm long.

E. praecox (Brittle Gum): found localised, Capertree district and Captains Flat, New South Wales.
Buds pedicellate, glaucous.

3 **Fruit** medium sized, 0.6-0.8 cm long.
E. elliptica (Bendemeer Gum): found from Nandewar Range and Armidale to Tomalla, New South Wales. Q
Buds pedicellate, glaucous.

CHAPTER 5 DOUBLE-CAPPED EUCALYPTS

Manna Gums and Others

Group characteristics
Juvenile leaves opposite, sessile.
Adult leaves concolourous.
Inflorescences axillary, simple, pedunculate.
Buds scarred.

Division of the Manna Gums into species
1 **Fruit** cupular to campanulate; discs flat to slightly raised; valves exsert.

   2 **Buds** sessile to sub-sessile, in threes; hypanthia cylindrical; opercula flat, beaked.

   3 **Juvenile leaves** lanceolate, dull, grey-green.

   6 **Fruit** medium sized, to 0.9 cm wide.
   E. wilcoxii: mallee, found isolated spots, Wadbilliga and Deua National Parks, New South Wales.
   bark gum.
   Adult leaves narrow-lanceolate, dull, green.

   3 **Juvenile leaves** broad-lanceolate, dull, green.

   6 **Fruit** medium size to large, to 1 cm wide.
   E. baeuerlenii (Baeuerlen's Gum): mallee, found Wentworth Falls, Blue Mountains, Mount Budawang and Sugarloaf Mountain, southern New South Wales.
   bark gum.
   Adult leaves lanceolate, dull, green.

   2 **Buds** sessile, in sevens, ovoid.

   3 **Juvenile leaves** lanceolate, cordate, dull, green.

   4 **Bark** compact, on lower trunk.

   6 **Fruit** small, to 0.5 cm wide.
   E. badjensis (Big Badja Gum): medium to tall forest tree, found Big Badja Hill to Cathcart, southern tableland, New South Wales.
   Adult leaves narrow-lanceolate, dull, green.

   3 **Juvenile leaves** broad-lanceolate to ovate, cordate, dull, green.

   4 **Bark** fibrous, tending peppermint, to large branches.

   6 **Fruit** small, to 0.6 cm wide.
   E. macarthurii (Camden Woollybutt): medium sized tree, found from Boyd to Paddy's Rivers, central tableland, New South Wales.
   Adult leaves narrow-lanceolate, dull, green.

1 continued on next page.

1 **Fruit** small to medium sized, to 0.8 cm wide, globular; disc raised; valves exsert.
  2 **Buds** pedicellate, in sevens.
    3 **Juvenile leaves** lanceolate, cordate, dull, green.
      4 **Bark** compact, to about mid trunk.

E. smithii (Gully Gum): mallee to tall forest tree, found central and southern tableland south from Yerranderie, New South Wales, and eastern Victoria.
Adult leaves narrow-lanceolate, glossy to semi-glossy, green.
Fruit usually small, to 0.5 cm wide.

  2 **Buds** sessile to subsessile, in threes or sevens, ovoid to double conical.
    3 **Juvenile leaves** lanceolate to broad-lanceolate, dull, green.
      4 **Bark** rough, to the large branches or higher.
        5 **Buds** mainly in sevens.

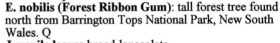

E. viminalis ssp cygnetensis (Rough-barked Manna Gum): small to medium sized tree, found Kangaroo Island, southern tip of Eyre Peninsula, south-eastern South Australia, and south-western Victoria.
Juvenile leaves lanceolate.
Adult leaves narrow-lanceolate to lanceolate, glossy, green.

        5 **Buds** mainly in threes.

E. pryoriana (Gippsland Manna Gum): small to medium sized tree, found on sandy soil, southern Victoria.
Juvenile leaves lanceolate.
Adult leaves narrow-lanceolate, glossy, green.

      4 **Bark** gum, or basal plates.
        5 **Buds** mainly in sevens.

E. nobilis (Forest Ribbon Gum): tall forest tree found north from Barrington Tops National Park, New South Wales. Q
Juvenile leaves broad-lanceolate.
Adult leaves narrow-lanceolate to lanceolate, glossy, green.

        5 **Buds** mainly in threes, rarely sevens.

E. viminalis ssp. viminalis (Manna or Ribbon Gum): medium to very tall tree, found widely and frequently along creeks; tablelands New South Wales, mountains and southern parts Victoria, south-east and the Lofty Ranges, South Australia, central and eastern Tasmania. Q
Juvenile leaves lanceolate.
Adult leaves narrow-lanceolate to lanceolate, glossy, green.

    3 continued next page.

3 **Juvenile leaves** orbicular to ovate, dull, grey-green to green.
  4 **Bark** gum, or basal plates.
    E. dalrympleana (Mountain Gum): medium sized tree
    Adult leaves narrow-lanceolate to lanceolate, glossy, green.
      5 **Buds** mainly in sevens.

        ssp. heptantha: found north from Niangala, New South Wales. Q
        Fruit mainly medium sized, to 0.7 cm wide; hypanthia campanulate.

      5 **Buds** mainly in threes.
        ssp. dalrympleana: found mountain areas; south from Ilford, New South Wales, eastern Victoria, Tasmania. Large fruit and large leaf form found at Falls Creek, Victoria.

3 **Juvenile leaves** glaucous.
  4 **Bark** gum, or basal plates, orange to yellow patches.
    E. rubida (Candlebark): medium to tall forest tree.
    Adult leaves narrow-lanceolate to lanceolate, dull, grey-green to green.
      5 **Buds** mainly in threes.
        6 **Juvenile leaves** orbicular, mainly <5 cm wide.
        ssp. rubida: found on mountains and tablelands; south from Kandos, New South Wales, Victoria, Tasmania, Lofty Ranges, South Australia.

        6 **Juvenile leaves** orbicular, >5 cm wide, stems squared.
        ssp. canobolensis: found Mount Canobolas, New South Wales.

        6 **Juvenile leaves** ovate.
        ssp. barbigerorum: found Glen Innes to Guyra to Tingha, New South Wales.

      5 **Buds** mainly in sevens.
        6 **Juvenile leaves** orbicular, mainly <5 cm wide.
        ssp. septemflora: found Mount Beauty, Victoria, and just into southern New South Wales

CHAPTER 5 DOUBLE-CAPPED EUCALYPTS

BOXES and IRONBARKS

The Boxes and Ironbarks are divided into two groups by the flower structure.

Narrow-flowered Boxes and Ironbarks
    They have narrow flowers with all the stamens having anthers and usually the opercula scars at the widest part of the buds. They can be further divided into scarred or non-scarred species.
Scarred Narrow-flowered Boxes (page 78)
Scarred Narrow-flowered Ironbarks (page 80)
Non-scarred, Narrow-flowered Boxes
        Grey Boxes (page 82)
        Mallee Boxes (page 83)

Broad-flowered Boxes and Ironbarks
    They have broad flowers with staminodes and the hypanthia wider than the opercula. They can be further subdivided into scarred and non-scarred species.
Scarred Broad-flowered Boxes (page 86)
Scarred Broad-flowered Ironbarks (page 88)
Non-scarred Broad-flowered Box and Ironbarks (page 90)

Division of the Boxes.
1 **Buds** scarred.

    2 **Opercula** about equal width to **hypanthia**. (stamens all have anthers)
        Scarred Narrow-flowered Box (page 78) NSW VIC SA

    2 **Hypanthia** wider than **opercula.**
        3 Partial box barked trees. (stamens all have anthers)
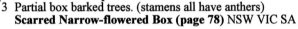
            Scarred Narrow-flowered Box (page 78) NSW VIC SA

        3 Fully box or gum barked trees.
            5 **Juvenile leaves** linear. (stamens all have anthers)
              E. largiflorens (Black Box) (page 79) NSW VIC SA

            5 **Juvenile leaves** ovate. (staminodes present)
              Scarred Broad-flowered Box (page 86) NSW VIC SA

1 **Buds** not scarred.
        3 Mallees. (stamens all have anthers)
            Mallee Box (page 83) NSW VIC SA

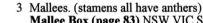
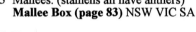

        3 Trees.

            4 **Fruit** square in cross section (four angles) (stamens all have anthers)
              E. froggattii (Kamarooka Mallee) (page 85) VIS

            4 **Fruit**; valves up to six. (stamens all have anthers)
              E. bosistoana (Coast Grey Box) (page 83) NSW VIC

            4 continued on next page.

4 **Fruit** rims thick; valves up to five.

7 **Adult leaves** glossy. (stamens all have anthers)
E. porosa (South Australian Mallee Box) (page 83) NSW VIC SA

7 **Adult leaves** dull. (staminodes present)
E. melliodora (Yellow Box) (page 90) NSW VIC
Note - rims of fruit have rings of dark tissue that can be lost when old. If in doubt cut open a bud and check for staminodes.

4 **Fruit**; rims thin; valves up to five. (stamens all have anthers)
6 **Buds** mainly terminal, compound.
8 **Adult leaves** glossy.
Mallee Box (page 83) SA

8 **Adult leaves** dull.
Grey Box (page 82) NSW VIC SA

6 **Buds** mainly axillary, simple.
Mallee Box (page 83) NSW VIC SA

Division of the Ironbarks

1 **Buds** scarred; **inflorescences** mainly terminal, compound.
2 **Bark** Ironbark.

3 **Opercula** equal width to hypanthia. (stamens all have anthers)
Scarred Narrow-flowered Ironbark (page 80) NSW

3 **Opercula** narrower than hypanthia.

4 **Fruit** medium sized, to 0.8 cm long, conical to slightly cupular; valves weakly exsert; **Adult leaves** concolourous. (stamens all have anthers)
E. siderophloia (Ironbark) (page 81) NSW

4 **Fruit** not as above or **Adult leaves** discolourous. (staminodes present)
Scarred Broad-flowered Ironbark (page 88) NSW

1 **Buds** not scarred; **inflorescences** axillary, simple. (staminodes present)
2 **Bark** ironbark.
Red Ironbark (page 90) NSW VIC

2 **Bark** gum.
Yellow Gum (page 91) VIC SA

CHAPTER 5 DOUBLE-CAPPED EUCALYPTS

Scarred Narrow-flowered Boxes

Group characteristics
Juvenile leaves alternate, petiolate.
Inflorescences mainly terminal, compound.
Buds scarred, in sevens (rarely threes), pedicellate; opercula usually equal width to hypanthia; stamens all have anthers.

Division of the Narrow-flowered Boxes into species
1 **Bark** box, on lower trunk, trunk or to large branches.
    2 **Fruit** small to 0.5 cm long, hemispherical, thin walled; valves strongly exsert.

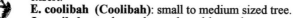

    E. coolibah (Coolibah): small to medium sized tree.
    Juvenile leaves lanceolate to broad-lanceolate, grey-green to glaucous.
    Adult leaves narrow-lanceolate to lanceolate, dull, grey-green, concolourous.

        5 **Buds** ovoid to fusiform, glaucous.
        ssp. coolibah: found on heavy soil, north from Wilcannia and east to Narrabri, New South Wales. Q NT

        5 **Buds** ovoid to fusiform, green; opercula conical.
        ssp. exserta: found Moree to Goondiwindi, New South Wales. Q NT

        5 **Buds** ovoid to fusiform, green; opercula rounded.
        ssp. arida: found north-west from Menindee, New South Wales. Q NT

    2 **Fruit** medium sized, to 0.9 cm long, cupular to ovoid; discs depressed; rims thin.
    E. intertexta (Gum-barked Coolibah): small to medium sized tree, found west from Nyngan, western New South Wales, and northern South Australia. Q NT WA
    Juvenile leaves ovate to broad-lanceolate.
    Adult leaves narrow-lanceolate to lanceolate, dull, grey-green, concolourous.
    Buds ovoid to clavate; opercula conical, often little narrower than hypanthia.

    2 **Fruit** small, to 0.6 cm long, cupular, discs depressed; rims thick.
    E. behriana (Bull Mallee) mallee, found scattered spots in mallee regions; New South Wales, Victoria, South Australia, and near Bacchus Marsh, Victoria.
    Juvenile leaves alternate, petiolate, ovate, grey-green to glaucous.
    Adult leaves broad-lanceolate to ovate, dull to glossy, green, concolourous, leathery.
    Buds shortly pedicellate, clavate.

1 continued on next page.

1 **Bark** box, to at least large branches.
    2 **Fruit** small, to 0.5 cm long, cupular; discs depressed; rims thin.

        3 **Leaves** at maturity broad-lanceolate to ovate, concolourous.
           E. populnea ssp. bimbil (Bimble Box): small to medium sized tree, found widespread, north from Narrandera and Pooncarie, western New South Wales. Q
           Juvenile leaves ovate to orbicular, glossy, green, found at maturity.
           Adult leaves broad-lanceolate, glossy, green, rarely found.
           Buds ovoid.

        3 **Leaves** at maturity lanceolate or narrower, concolourous.
           4 **Juvenile leaves** lanceolate to broad-lanceolate, dull, green.
             E. largeana (Craven Grey Box): medium to tall forest tree, found Gloucester, Craven and Pokolbin, New South Wales.
             Adult leaves narrow-lanceolate, dull, green.
             Buds ovoid.
             E rudderi (page 86) may key out as **E. largeana**. Check site or cut open bud and check for presence of staminodes.

           4 **Juvenile leaves** linear, grey-green to glaucous.
             E. largiflorens (Black Box): small to medium sized tree, found on heavy soil near lakes and streams; western New South Wales, north-western Victoria; eastern South Australia. Q
             Adult leaves narrow-lanceolate to lanceolate, dull, grey-green; venation acute.
             Buds ovoid; opercula often little narrower than hypanthia.

        3 **Leaves** at maturity lanceolate, discolourous.
         E. rummeryi (Steel Box or Brown Box): medium to tall forest tree, found from Dorrigo to Casino, New South Wales.
         Juvenile leaves broad-lanceolate to ovate, dull, green.
         Adult leaves lanceolate, dull, green, discolourous.
         Buds ovoid.
          E. hypostomatica (page 86) may key out as **E. rummeryi**. Check site or cut open bud and check for presence of staminodes.

1 **Bark** gum.
    2 **Fruit** small, to 0.6 cm long, conical; discs depressed; rims thin.
      E. dawsonii (Slaty Box) small to medium sized tree, found upper Hunter Valley, New South Wales.

      Juvenile leaves ovate to orbicular, dull, grey-green.
      Adult leaves lanceolate, concolourous, dull, grey-green.
      Buds ovoid to fusiform, glaucous.

Scarred Narrow-flowered Ironbarks

Group Characteristics
Bark ironbark, to at least large branches.
Juvenile leaves dull.
Adult leaves concolourous.
Inflorescences mainly terminal, compound.
Buds scarred, in sevens or more, pedicellate; stamen all have anthers.

Division of the Narrow-flowered Ironbarks into species
1 **Leaves** at maturity alternate, petiolate.
> 2 **Buds** fusiform; opercula high conical to horned; equal width to hypanthia.
>> 3 **Juvenile leaves** alternate, petiolate, ovate to orbicular, green.
>>> 4 **Fruit** medium to large, to 1.2 cm long, conical to pyriform; discs flat to ascending; valves flat to exsert.
>>> **E. fibrosa (Broad-leaved Ironbark)**: medium sized tree, found on coast and nearby hills, north from Moruya, New South Wales. Q
>>> **Bark** often flaky.
>>> **Adult leaves** lanceolate to broad-lanceolate, dull, green or grey-green.

> 2 **Buds** fusiform, glaucous; opercula high conical, equal width to the hypanthia.
>> 3 **Juvenile leaves** alternate, petiolate, orbicular to ovate, glaucous.
>>> 4 **Fruit** medium sized to large, to 1.1 cm long, conical to hemispherical; discs flat; valves flat to exsert.
>>> **E. nubila (Blue-leaved Ironbark)**: medium sized tree, found north from Dubbo, New South Wales. Q
>>> **Adult leaves** narrow-lanceolate to lanceolate, dull, grey-green to glaucous.

> 2 **Buds** clavate, opercula cylindrical, round ended, equal width to hypanthia.
>> 3 **Juvenile leaves** alternate, petiolate, ovate to orbicular, glaucous.
>>> 4 **Fruit** medium sized, to 0.7 cm long, conical to hemispherical; discs flat to raised; valves exsert.
>>> **E. ophitica**: small tree, found near Baryulgil north of Grafton, New South Wales.
>>> **Adult leaves** lanceolate, dull, grey-green to glaucous.

1 and 2 continued on next page.

2 **Buds** double conical to fusiform; hypanthia a little wider than opercula.
   3 **Juvenile leaves** alternate, petiolate, broad lanceolate to ovate, dull, green.

      4 **Fruit** medium sized, 0.8 cm long, conical to cupular; discs depressed; valves flat to slightly exsert.
      E. siderophloia (Northern Grey Ironbark): medium to tall tree, found New South Wales coast, north from Sydney. Q
      Adult leaves lanceolate to broad-lanceolate, dull, green or grey-green.

2 **Buds** ovoid; opercula equal width to hypanthia.
   3 **Juvenile leaves** alternate, petiolate, linear to narrow-lanceolate, dull, green or grey-green.

      4 **Fruit** small to medium sized, to 0.7 cm long, cupular; discs depressed; rims thin.
      E. crebra (Narrow-leaved Ironbark): medium sized tree, found central coast and northern western slopes, north from Picton, New South Wales. Q
      Adult leaves narrow-lanceolate to lanceolate, dull, green to grey-green.

1 **Leaves** at maturity opposite, sessile.
  2 **Buds** ovoid to fusiform, glaucous; opercula equal width to hypanthia.
    3 **Juvenile leaves** opposite, sessile, ovate to orbicular, cordate, glaucous.

      4 **Fruit** medium sized, to 0.8 cm long, cupular; discs flat; rims thin.
      E. melanophloia (Silver-leaved Ironbark): small to medium sized tree, found western slopes, north from Dubbo, New South Wales. Q
      Adult leaves when formed opposite, sub-sessile, broad-lanceolate to ovate, glaucous.

CHAPTER 5 DOUBLE-CAPPED EUCALYPTS

Grey Boxes (Non-scarred Narrow-flowered Boxes)

Group Characteristics
Small to medium sized trees.
Juvenile leaves alternate, petiolate, dull.
Adult leaves concolourous.
Inflorescences mainly terminal, compound.
Buds non-scarred, in sevens; stamens all have anthers.
Fruit; discs depressed; rims thin.

Division of the Grey Boxes into species.
1 **Bark** box, on part to all of trunk.
   2 **Adult leaves** narrow-lanceolate, dull, green.
      3 **Fruit** large to 1.8 cm long, cylindrical to ovoid.
      E. ochrophloia (Yapunyah): found Paroo River, north-western New South Wales. Q
      Juvenile leaves lanceolate, green.
      Buds pedicellate, fusiform.

   2 **Adult leaves** lanceolate to broad-lanceolate, glossy, green.
      3 **Fruit** medium sized, to 0.9 cm long, ovoid.
      E. moluccana (Grey Box): found coast and nearby hills, north from Nowra, New South Wales. Q
      Juvenile leaves ovate to orbicular, green.
      Buds pedicellate, fusiform.

1 **Bark** box, to large branches.
   2 **Adult leaves** narrow-lanceolate to lanceolate, dull, green.
      3 **Fruit** small to medium sized, to 0.7 cm long, cupular to ovoid.
      E. microcarpa (Grey Box): found widespread; west from Mudgee, New South Wales, northern Victoria and several isolated spots Flinders and Lofty Ranges, South Australia. Q
      Buds pedicellate, ovoid to fusiform.
      Juvenile leaves ovate, green.

   2 **Adult leaves** linear to narrow-lanceolate, glossy, green to grey-green.
      3 **Fruit** small, to 0.5 cm long, cupular.
      E. pilligaensis (Narrow-leaved Grey Box): found western slopes, north from Gilgandra, New South Wales. Q
      Juvenile leaves linear, grey-green.
      Buds pedicellate, ovoid to fusiform.

   2 **Adult leaves** lanceolate to broad-lanceolate, dull, grey-green to glaucous.

      3 **Fruit** large, to 1.5 cm long, ovoid to urceolate, angular, glaucous.
      E. albens (White Box): found widely tablelands and western slopes, New South Wales, and into north-eastern Victoria. Q
      Buds sessile or pedicellate, fusiform, angular, glaucous.
      Juvenile leaves ovate to orbicular, glaucous.

CHAPTER 5 DOUBLE-CAPPED EUCALYPTS

Mallee Boxes (Non-scarred Narrow-flowered Boxes)

Group Characteristics
Juvenile leaves alternate, petiolate.
Adult leaves concolourous; venation tending acute.
Inflorescences pedunculate.
Buds in sevens or more; stamens all have anthers.
Fruit cupular to ovoid; discs depressed.

Division of the Mallee Boxes into species
1 **Inflorescences** mainly axillary, simple.
 2 **Fruit** medium sized, to 0.7 cm long; valves up to six.
  3 **Buds** non-scarred, pedicellate, ovoid to clavate.

   4 **Adult leaves** narrow-lanceolate to lanceolate, dull to semi-glossy, green.
   E. bosistoana (Coast Grey Box): medium to large tree, found south of Wolgan, New South Wales, eastern coast Victoria.
   Bark, box, to variable amount on the lower half of trunk.
   Juvenile leaves ovate to orbicular, dull, green.

 2 **Fruit** medium sized, to 0.7 cm long; rims thick.
  3 **Buds** non-scarred, pedicellate, ovoid.
   4 **Adult leaves** lanceolate, glossy, green; intramarginal vein about 3 mm. from leaf edge.
   E. porosa (South Australian Mallee Box): mallee to small tree, found mallee regions; New South Wales, Victoria, South Australia.
   Bark box, on trunk or to large branches.
   Juvenile leaves ovate, dull, green.

 2 **Fruit** medium sized, to 0.8 cm long; rims thin.
  3 **Buds** non-scarred, pedicellate, ovoid to fusiform, slightly angular; flowers white or pink.

   4 **Adult leaves** lanceolate, >1 cm wide, dull, grey-green.
   E. odorata ssp. odorata (Peppermint Box): mallee to medium sized tree, found Lofty and Flinders Ranges and south-east South Australia, and just into Victoria.
   Bark box, on trunk or on base of mallee.
   Juvenile leaves lanceolate, grey-green.

  3 **Buds** scarred, pedicellate, ovoid to fusiform; outer operculum comes off in scales.
   4 **Adult leaves** narrow-lanceolate, dull, grey-green.
   E. desquamata (Devil's Peak Box): mallee, found Devil's Peak near Quorn, South Australia.
   Bark gum, coppery.
   Juvenile leaves lanceolate, grey-green.

1 and 2 continued on next page.

2 **Fruit** small, to 0.6 cm long; rims thin.
  3 **Buds** non-scarred, pedicellate, ovoid to fusiform.

  4 **Adult leaves** linear, <0.8 cm wide, partially erect, glossy, green.
    5 **Juvenile leaves** subsessile, linear, dull, green.
    E. viridis (Green Mallee): mallee, found western slopes, central and northern New South Wales and in isolated areas, northern Victoria. Q
    Bark gum, or some basal box.

  4 **Adult leaves** narrow-lanceolate, >0.8 cm wide, glossy, grey-green.
    5 **Juvenile leaves** narrow-lanceolate, grey-green.
    E. wimmerensis (Wimmera mallee Box): mallee, found western Victoria, extending just into South Australia.
    Bark gum, or some basal box.

  4 **Adult leaves** narrow-lanceolate <1 cm wide, glossy, grey-green.
    5 **Juvenile leaves** lanceolate, grey-green.
    E. odorata ssp. augustifolia (Seaside Mallee Box): mallee, found Flinders Ranges and Eyre Peninsular, South Australia.
    Bark gum or some basal plates.

  4 **Adult leaves** linear to narrow-lanceolate, dull, blue-green.
    5 **Juvenile leaves** linear to narrow-lanceolate, sub-glaucous.
    E. polybractea (Blue-leaved Mallee): mallee, found near West Wyalong, New South Wales and Bendigo, Victoria.
    Bark gum, or some basal box.

  4 **Adult leaves** linear to narrow-lanceolate, glossy, green.
    5 **Juvenile leaves** linear to narrow-lanceolate, glaucous.
    E. species (Flinders Range Mallee Box): mallee found on ridge tops, Flinders Ranges, South Australia.
    Bark gum.

1 continued on next page.

1 **Inflorescences** mainly terminal compound.
  2 **Fruit** medium sized, to 0.8 cm long, cylindrical, square in cross section (four angles).
    3 **Buds** non-scarred, pedicellate, fusiform, square in cross section (four angles).

      4 **Adult leaves** lanceolate, glossy, green, leathery; intramarginal vein about 3 mm from leaf edge.
      E. froggattii (Kamarooka Mallee): mallee to small tree, found near Bendigo and Charlton, Victoria.
      Bark box, some longitudinal furrows.
      Juvenile leaves lanceolate, green.

  2 **Fruit** medium sized, to 0.8 cm long, ovoid; rims thin.
    3 **Buds** non-scarred, sessile, fusiform, faintly angular; flowers purple or white.

      4 **Adult leaves** lanceolate, glossy, green.
      E. lansdowneana ssp. albopurpurea (Purple-flowered Mallee Box) mallee to small tree, found Kangaroo Island and southern Eyre Peninsula, South Australia.
      Bark box, on stems of mallees, to large branches of trees.
      Juvenile leaves lanceolate to broad-lanceolate, green.

  2 **Fruit** medium to large, to 1 cm long, ovoid, angles; rims thin.
    3 **Buds** non-scarred, sessile, fusiform, angular; flowers crimson.
      4 **Adult leaves** lanceolate, glossy, green.
      E. lansdowneana ssp. lansdowneana (Crimson Mallee) mallee to small tree, found Gawler Range, South Australia.
      Bark box on stems of mallees, to large branches of trees.
      Juvenile leaves lanceolate to broad-lanceolate, green.

Scarred Broad-flowered Boxes

Group characteristics
Juvenile leaves alternate, petiolate.
> **Inflorescences** mainly terminal, compound.
> **Buds** scarred, in sevens, pedicellate, clavate to ovoid; opercula narrower than hypanthia; staminodes present.
> **Fruit**; discs depressed, rims thin.

Division of the Scarred Broad-flowered Boxes into species
1 **Leaves** at maturity broad-lanceolate or narrower.
> 2 **Bark** box, to at least large branches.
>> 3 **Fruit** small, to 0.5 cm long, cupular.
>>> 4 **Adult leaves** lanceolate to broad-lanceolate, dull, green, discolourous.
>>> **E. hypostomatica**: medium to tall forest tree, found coastal hills from Pokolbin to Kangaroo Valley, New South Wales.
>>> **Juvenile leaves** broad-lanceolate to ovate, dull, green.
>>> **E. rummeryi (page 79)** may key out as **E. hypostomatica**. Check site or cut open a bud and check for presence of staminodes.

>>> 4 **Adult leaves** narrow-lanceolate to lanceolate, dull, green, concolourous.
>>> **E. rudderi (Rudder's Box)**: medium to tall forest tree, found Taree-Karuah district, New South Wales.
>>> **Juvenile leaves** lanceolate to broad-lanceolate, dull, green.
>>> **E. largeana (page 79)** may key out as **E rudderi**. Check site or cut open a bud and check for presence of staminodes.

>> 3 **Fruit** medium sized, to 0.7 cm long, conical.
>> **E. conica (Fuzzy Box)**: medium sized tree, found western slopes, north from Wagga, New South Wales. Q
>> **Juvenile leaves** ovate, dull, green to grey-green.
>> **Adult leaves** narrow-lanceolate to lanceolate, dull, grey-green, concolourous.

> 2 **Bark** gum, some adherent flakes on trunk.
>> 3 **Fruit** medium sized, to 0.9 cm long, ovoid; rims thin.
>> **E. fasciculosa (Pink Gum)**: small to medium sized tree, found south-eastern South Australia including Kangaroo Island, and just into western Victoria..
>> **Juvenile leaves** ovate, dull, green.
>> **Adult leaves** lanceolate to broad-lanceolate, dull, green, concolourous.

1 continued on next page.

1 **Leaves** at maturity often orbicular to ovate.

       3 **Fruit** medium sized, to 0.7 cm long, cupular.
       E. polyanthemos (Red Box): small to medium sized tree.
       Juvenile leaves orbicular, dull, grey-green to glaucous.
       Adult leaves when formed broad-lanceolate, dull, grey-green to glaucous, concolourous.

           5 **Bark** gum, some adherent flakes on trunk.
           ssp. polyanthemos: found central tablelands, New South Wales.

           5 **Bark** box, to at least large branches.
           ssp. vestita: found central to eastern Victoria, Albury and Bombala New South Wales,

       3 **Fruit** medium sized, to 0.7 long, conical.
       E. bauerana (Blue Box): small to medium sized tree, found central and southern coast, south from Putty, New South Wales; eastern coast Victoria.
       Bark box, to at least large branches.
       Juvenile leaves orbicular, dull, green.
       Adult leaves when formed broad-lanceolate, semi-glossy, green to blue-green, concolourous.

       3 **Fruit** medium to large, to 1 cm long, conical.
       E. magnificata (Blue Box): small tree, found at Hillgrove, New South Wales. Q
       Bark box, to at least large branches.
       Juvenile leaves orbicular, dull, grey-green.
       Adult leaves when formed broad-lanceolate, semi-glossy, grey-green, concolourous.

CHAPTER 5 DOUBLE-CAPPED EUCALYPTS

Scarred Broad-flowered Ironbarks

Group Characteristics
Bark ironbark, to at least large branches.
Juvenile leaves alternate, petiolate.
Inflorescences mainly terminal, compound, pedicellate.
Buds scarred, pedicellate, in sevens; opercula narrower than hypanthia; staminodes
   present.

Division of Scarred Broad-flowered Ironbarks into species.
1 **Buds** ovoid to clavate, green.
      2 **Fruit** small to 0.6 cm long, cupular; discs depressed; rims thin.
            3 **Adult leaves** narrow-lanceolate to lanceolate, dull, green,

concolourous.
E. beyeriana (Beyer's Ironbark): small to medium sized tree, found
from Narrabri to Nowra, New South Wales.
Juvenile leaves narrow-lanceolate to lanceolate, dull, green.

1 **Buds** ovoid to fusiform, green.
      2 **Fruit** medium sized, to 0.9 cm long, cupular to pyriform; discs depressed;
         rims thick.
            3 **Adult leaves** lanceolate to broad-lanceolate, semi-glossy, green,

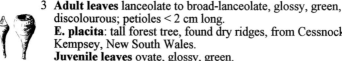

discolourous.
E. paniculata (Grey Ironbark)
Juvenile leaves ovate, dull or glossy, green.
                  5 Medium to tall forest tree, found coast and nearby hills
                     from Bulahdelah to Bermagui, New South Wales.
                     ssp. paniculata
                     Adult leaves; no stomata on upper surface.

                  5 Mallee to small tree, found coast near Port Stephens and
                     Newcastle, New South Wales.
                     ssp. matutina
                     Adult leaves; stomata on upper surface.

            3 **Adult leaves** lanceolate to broad-lanceolate, glossy, green,
               discolourous; petioles < 2 cm long.
               E. placita: tall forest tree, found dry ridges, from Cessnock to
               Kempsey, New South Wales.
               Juvenile leaves ovate, glossy, green.

            3 **Adult leaves** lanceolate, glossy, green, faintly discolourous to
               concolourous; petioles >2 cm long.
               E. ancophila: tall rain forest tree, found near Kempsey, New South
               Wales.
               Juvenile leaves lanceolate to broad-lanceolate, glossy, green.

1 and 2 continued on next page.

2 **Fruit** medium sized, to 0.7 cm long, hemispherical; discs depressed; rims thick.

    3 **Adult leaves** lanceolate to broad-lanceolate, dull, grey-green, concolourous.

    E. panda (Tumbledown Ironbark): small tree, found near Yetman, New South wales. Q

    Juvenile leaves lanceolate to broad-lanceolate, dull, green.

2 **Fruit** large, to 1.3 cm long, conical to pyriform; discs depressed; rims thin.

    3 **Adult leaves** lanceolate to broad-lanceolate, semi-glossy, green, discolourous.

    E. fusiformis: a medium sized forest tree, found north from Kempsey, New South Wales. Q

    Juvenile leaves ovate, dull or glossy, green.

1 **Buds** fusiform, square in cross section (four angles), green.

  2 **Fruit** conical, square in cross; discs depressed; rims thick.

    3 **Adult leaves** lanceolate to broad-lanceolate, dull, green, concolourous.

    E. tetrapleura (Square-fruited Ironbark): medium sized tree, found near Grafton, New South Wales.

    Juvenile leaves broad-lanceolate to ovate, dull, green.

    Fruit medium sized, to 1 cm long.

    3 **Adult leaves** lanceolate, grey-green, dull, discolourous.

    E. fergusonii: medium sized tree.

    Juvenile leaves lanceolate, dull, green.

      4 **Fruit** large, to 1.3 cm long.

      ssp. dorsiventralis: found near Wollombi, New South Wales.

      Adult leaves; no stomata on upper surface.

      4 **Fruit** medium sized, to 1 cm long.

      ssp. fergusonii: found from Morisset to Bulahdelah, New South Wales.

      Adult leaves; stomata on upper surface.

1 **Buds** ovoid to clavate, square or round, glaucous.

  2 **Fruit** medium sized, to 1 cm long, ovoid; discs depressed; rims thin.

    3 **Adult leaves** lanceolate to broad-lanceolate, glaucous, concolourous.

    E. caleyi (Caley's Ironbark): small to medium sized tree.

    Inflorescences often axillary, simple.

    Juvenile leaves ovate to orbicular, glaucous, often at maturity.

      4 **Fruit** round.

      ssp. caleyi: found north from Goulburn River, northern and central tablelands, New South Wales. Q

      4 **Fruit** square in cross section (four angles).

      ssp. ovendenii: found west of Tenterfield, New South Wales.

CHAPTER 5 DOUBLE-CAPPED EUCALYPTS

Non-scarred Broad-flowered Box and Ironbarks

E. melliodora (Yellow Box): medium sized tree, found widespread, tablelands and inland slopes New South Wales; Gippsland, western, central, north-eastern Victoria. Q
Bark box, for a variable amount on trunk, grey, yellow, red brown or black, dense or loose, yellow gum above.
Juvenile leaves alternate, petiolate, ovate, dull, grey-green or green.
Adult leaves narrow-lanceolate to lanceolate, dull, green or grey-green, concolourous.
Inflorescences mainly axillary, simple, pedunculate.
Buds non-scarred, in sevens, pedicellate, ovoid; opercula weakly beaked; staminodes present.
Fruit medium sized, to 0.7 cm long, cupular; discs depressed; rims often have black rings.

Red Ironbarks

Group Characteristics
Medium to tall trees.
Bark ironbark, to at least large branches.
Juvenile leaves alternate, petiolate.
Adult leaves lanceolate, concolourous.

Inflorescences axillary, simple; peduncles long.
Buds non-scarred, ovoid; pedicels long; staminodes present; flowers white or pink.
Fruit cupular; discs depressed; rims often have black rings.

Division Red Ironbarks into species
1 **Buds** in sevens.
E. sideroxylon (Mugga): found western slopes, New South Wales, and just into north-eastern Victoria. Q
Juvenile leaves linear to lanceolate, dull, green to glaucous.
Adult leaves dull, green to grey-green.
Fruit medium sized, to 1 cm wide.

1 **Buds** in threes.
E. tricarpa (Red Ironbark): found south New South Wales coast south from Araluen, east Gippsland, central Victoria,
Juvenile leaves broad-lanceolate to ovate, dull, green.
Adult leaves dull, green.
Fruit large, to 1.4 cm wide.

CHAPTER 5 DOUBLE-CAPPED EUCALYPTS

Yellow Gums

Group Characteristics
Bark gum, often basal plates.
Juvenile leaves dull
Adult leaves dull, concolourous.

Inflorescences axillary, simple, pedunculate.
Buds non-scarred, in threes, ovoid, pedicellate; staminodes present; flowers white or pink.
Fruit hemispherical, cupular or cylindrical; discs depressed; rims often have black rings.

Division of the Yellow Gums into subspecies
1 **Juvenile leaves** opposite, sessile.
   E. leucoxylon
      2 **Juvenile leaves** never connate, green; **Buds** green.
         3 **Fruit** medium to large, to 1 cm wide, (larger on Kangaroo Island), longer than wide.
            4 **Adult leaves** narrow-lanceolate to lanceolate, green.
            ssp. leucoxylon (Yellow Gum): small to medium sized tree, found south-western Victoria, Fleurieu Peninsula, Kangaroo Island and south of Port Pirie, South Australia.
            Juvenile leaves broad-lanceolate to ovate, cordate.

         3 **Fruit** large, to 1.4 cm wide, longer than wide.
            4 **Adult leaves** lanceolate to broad-lanceolate, green.
            ssp. megalocarpa (Large-fruited Yellow Gum): mallee to small tree, found near Mount Gambia, South Australia.
            Juvenile leaves broad-lanceolate to ovate, cordate.

         3 **Fruit** medium to large, to 1.1 cm wide, wider than long; valves covered with white tissue.
            4 **Adult leaves** narrow-lanceolate to lanceolate, green.
            ssp. stephaniae (Desert Yellow Gum): mallee to small tree, found Little Desert National park, Victoria and into south-eastern South Australia.
            Juvenile leaves lanceolate to ovate.

      2 **Juvenile leaves** often connate, green; **Buds** green.
         3 **Fruit** medium to large, to 1.1 cm wide, wider than long.
            4 **Adult leaves** lanceolate, green.
            ssp. connata (Melbourne Yellow Gum): medium sized tree, found Studley Park, Brisbane Range and Anglesea, Victoria.
            Juvenile leaves ovate, cordate.

1 and 2 continued on next page.

    2 **Juvenile leaves** often connate, glaucous; **Buds** glaucous.
       3 **Fruit** medium to large, to 1.4 cm wide, wider than long.
         4 **Adult leaves** narrow-lanceolate to lanceolate, grey-green.
          ssp. pruinosa (Inland Blue Gum): mallee to small tree, found central and western Victoria; Southern Flinders and Lofty Ranges and southern South Australia; south west New South Wales.
          Juvenile leaves ovate, cordate.

1 **Juvenile leaves** alternate, petiolate.
    2 **Juvenile leaves** never connate, green; **Buds** angular, green.
       3 **Fruit** large, to 1.4 cm wide, angular, longer than wide; discs covering valves.
         4 **Adult leaves** lanceolate, green.
          E. petiolaris (Eyre Peninsula Blue Gum): a small tree, found Eyre Peninsula, South Australia.
          Juvenile leaves broad-lanceolate to ovate.

CHAPTER 6 SINGLE-CAPPED EUCALYPTS

The **Single-capped Eucalypts** are the non-scarred Eucalypts after the exclusion of the non-scarred Bloodwoods, non-scarred Boxes and non-scarred Ironbarks.
The Single-capped Eucalypts can be divided groups.

The **Covered-valves Eucalypts (Series Diversifoliae) (page 95)** are mainly a Western Australia group that have wide discs that cover the valves. Only one species E. diversifolia (Soap Mallee) is found in South-eastern Australia.

The **White Mahoganies (Series Acmenoideae) (page 96)** are fully barked with stringybark that is less furrowed than usual and has medium length fibres. They have juvenile leaves that are at first opposite and sessile then subopposite and shortly petiolate and adult leaves that are either discolourous or leathery.

The **Stringybarks (Series Capitellatae) (page 97)** are usually, but not always fully barked with stringybark. Identification can be confirmed by the juvenile leaves being alternate, petiolate, undulate, and rough.

The **Blackbutts (Series Pilulares) (page 106)** have bark that is partial and stringybark that is less furrowed than usual and has medium length fibres. They have juvenile leaves that are opposite and sessile.

The **Peppermints (Series piperitae) (page 107)** have bark that is peppermint, compact or gum. They have juvenile leaves that are usually opposite and sessile.

The **Ashes (Series Obliquae) (page 111)** have juvenile leaves that are alternate, petiolate and smooth.

Division of the Single-capped Eucalypts.
1 **Inflorescences** non-pedunculate.
2 **Fruit** large, to 1.4 cm wide, hemispherical; discs wide, raised; valves exsert.
5 **Bark** gum.
E. deuaensis (Mongamulla Gum) (page 104) NSW

2 **Fruit** large, to 1.5 cm wide, globular, warty; rims distal to the widest point; valves exsert.
5 **Bark** box.
E. alpina (Grampians Gum, eastern form) (page 105) VIC

2 **Fruit** large, to 1.8 cm wide, hemispherical, warty; discs wide; valves exsert.
5 **Bark** stringybark.
E. alpina (Grampians Gum, western form) (page 105) VIC

1 continued on next page.

1 **Inflorescences** pedunculate.
    2 **Fruit** large, to 1.5 cm wide, hemispherical; discs wide, flat, covering valves.
        5 **Bark** gum.

           E. diversifolia (Soap Mallee) (page 95) VIC SA

    2 **Fruit** large to very large, 1.5 to 2.5 cm long, ovoid, ribbed; discs depressed.
        5 **Bark** compact, basal.
        E. olsenii (Woila Gum) (Page 105)

        5 **Bark** fine patterned, spongy, prickly to touch.
        E. planchoniana (Needlebark Stringybark)
                            (page 117) NSW

    2 **Fruit** not as above.
        3 **Buds** in more than seven, sessile, fusiform (stellate cluster).
           5 **Bark** gum or basal compact.
           Black Sallies (page 116) NSW VIC

           5 **Bark** stringybark.
           Stringybark (page 97) NSW VIC

        3 **Buds** not as above.
           4 **Juvenile leaves** opposite, sessile, smooth.
               5 **Bark** stringybark, on trunk or to large branches, less
                    furrowed than usual, medium length fibres.
               Blackbutt (page 106) NSW

               5 **Bark** gum, peppermint or compact.
               Peppermint (page 107) NSW VIC SA TAS

        4 and 5 continued on next page.

5 **Bark** stringybark, to small branches, less furrowed than usual, medium length fibres.
White Mahogany (page 96) NSW

4 **Juvenile leaves** alternate, or early ones opposite, petiolate, early ones rough.
5 **Bark** stringybark.

8 **Fruit** globular to hemispherical.
Stringybark (page 97) NSW VIC
SA

4 **Juvenile leaves** alternate, petiolate, smooth.
6 **Adult leaves** linear to narrow-lanceolate.
7 Tasmania.
Peppermint (page 107) TAS

7 Mainland
Ash (page 111) NSW VIC

6 **Adult leaves** not linear to narrow-lanceolate; venation acute.
Ash (page 111) NSW VIC SA TAS

6 **Adult leaves** not linear to narrow-lanceolate; venation not acute, tending transverse.
White Mahogany (page 96) NSW

COVERED-VALVES EUCALYPT

E. diversifolia (Soap Mallee): mallee, found limestone soils, exposed coastal sites; South Australia, western Victoria.
Bark gum, grey to light brown.
Juvenile leaves opposite to alternate, sessile to petiolate, ovate, dull, green.
Adult leaves lanceolate, leathery, dull, grey-green, erect, concolourous; venation acute.
Inflorescences axillary, simple, pedunculate.
Buds non-scarred, in sevens or more, pedicellate, double conical.
Fruit large, to 1.5 cm wide, hemispherical; discs wide, flat, covering valves.

95

WHITE MAHOGANIES

Group characteristics
Bark stringybark, less furrowed than usual, medium length fibres.
Juvenile leaves opposite to alternate, sessile to petiolate.
Inflorescences axillary, occasionally terminal, simple, occasionally compound, pedunculate.

Buds non-scarred, in sevens or more, pedicellate, ovoid to fusiform; opercula weakly beaked.

Division of the White Mahoganies into species
1 **Fruit** medium sized, to 0.7 cm wide, globular; discs depressed; rims thin.

  2 **Adult leaves** lanceolate to broad-lanceolate, glossy, green, strongly discolourous.
E. acmenoides (White Mahogany): tall tree, found better soils on ridges, coast north from Sydney, New South Wales. Q
Juvenile leaves broad-lanceolate, glossy, green.

  2 **Adult leaves** narrow-lanceolate to lanceolate, glossy, green, faintly discolourous.
E. apathalassica (Inland White Mahogany): medium sized tree, found at Yetman, New South Wales. Q
Juvenile leaves broad-lanceolate to ovate, glossy to dull, green.

1 **Fruit** medium sized, to 0.9 cm wide, hemispherical; disc wide; valves weakly exsert. .

  2 **Adult leaves** lanceolate, semi-glossy, green, concolourous, leathery.
E. umbra (Broad-leaved White Mahogany): small to medium sized tree, found poor soils on ridges, north of Sydney. Q
Juvenile leaves broad-lanceolate, glossy, green.

  2 **Adult leaves** narrow-lanceolate to lanceolate, semi-glossy to glossy, green, faintly discolourous.
E. psammitica (Broad-leaved White Mahogany): small to medium sized tree, found near Grafton, New South Wales.
Juvenile leaves narrow-lanceolate to broad-lanceolate, glossy to dull, green.

1 **Fruit** medium sized, to 0.9 cm wide, hemispherical, discs wide, slightly to moderately descending, rims thin.
  2 **Adult leaves** lanceolate to broad-lanceolate, dull, grey-green, concolourous, leathery.
E. carnea (Broad-leaved White Mahogany): small to medium sized tree, found poor soils, coast north from Hunter River, New South Wales. Q
Juvenile leaves broad-lanceolate, dull, grey-green.

CHAPTER 6 SINGLE-CAPPED EUCALYPTS

STRINGYBARKS

The Stringybarks can be divided into groups according to the colour of the wood in the major species of each group. The shape and size of their fruit is an aid in this division.

 Yellow Stringybark (page 98); fruit usually large, pedicellate; rims distal to widest point; adult leaves strongly discolourous.

 Red Stringybarks (page 99); fruit usually large, pedicellate or sessile; rims at widest point; valves exsert; adult leaves concolourous.

 White Stringybarks (page 100); fruit small to medium sized, shortly pedicellate to sessile; rims usually distal to wides point; leaves concolourous or slightly discolourous.

 Brown Stringybarks (page 103); fruit medium to large, sessile; rims distal to widest point; valves weakly exsert; adult leaves leathery, concolourous.

Division of the Stringybarks
1 **Fruit** clearly pedicellate; cluster open.
   2 **Adult leaves** strongly discolourous.
       3 **Fruit**; rims distal to widest point; discs flat; valves flat.
         4 **Buds** clavate; opercula low conical.
         Yellow Stringybark (page 98) NSW VIC

   2 **Adult leaves** concolourous or weakly discolourous.
       3 **Fruit**; rims at widest point; discs wide, raised; valves exsert.
         4 **Buds** angular or round.
         Red Stringybark (page 99) NSW VIC SA

      3 **Fruit**; rims distal to widest point; discs wide, flat or raised; valves exsert.
         4 **Buds** round.
         Red Stringybark (page 99) NSW VIC

         4 **Buds** angular.
         E. prominula (page 100) NSW

       3 **Fruit**; rims distal to widest point; discs wide, raised; valves flat or weakly exsert.
         4 **Buds** ovoid to fusiform, angular or round.
         White Stringybark (page 100) NSW

·1,   3 and 4 continued on next page.

        4 **Buds** clavate, round; opercula low conical or hemispherical.
         E. laevopinea (page 99) NSW

    3 **Fruit**; rims distal to widest point; discs narrow; valves flat.
     White Stringybark (page 100) NSW

1 **Fruit** sessile (fruit cluster crowded).

    3 **Fruit**; rims at widest point; discs wide, raised; valves exsert.
        4 **Buds** angular.
         Red Stringybark (page 99) NSW VIC SA

    3 **Fruit**; rims distal to widest point; discs wide, raised; valves exsert.
        4 **Buds** ovoid to fusiform, round.
         E. mckintii (East Gippsland Stringybark) (page 100) VIC

        4 **Buds** clavate, round; opercula low conical.
         E. blaxlandii (Blaxland's Stringybark) (page 104) NSW

    3 **Fruit**; rims distal to widest point; discs wide, raised; valves flat or
     weakly exsert.
        4 **Buds** ovoid to fusiform, round.
           5 **Fruit** compressed (flat surfaces of contact).
           Brown Stringybark (page 103) NSW VIC

           Fruit not compressed.
           E. tindaliae (Tindale's Stringybark) (page 101) NSW

        4 **Buds** clavate, round; opercula hemispherical to low conical,
         warty; or buds ovoid to fusiform, angular.
         Brown Stringybark (page 103) NSW VIC SA

    3 **Fruit**; rims distal to widest point; discs narrow; valves flat or weakly
     exsert.
     White Stringybark (page 100) NSW

Yellow Stringybark

E. muelleriana (Yellow Stringybark) tall forest tree, found coast and nearby hills;
south from Wollongong, New South Wales, eastern Victoria.
Bark stringybark.
Juvenile leaves alternate, petiolate, broad-lanceolate, glossy, green; very early ones
rough.
Adult leaves lanceolate to broad-lanceolate, falcate, semi-glossy, green, discolourous;
   venation acute.

Inflorescences axillary, simple, pedunculate.
Buds non-scarred, in sevens or more, pedicellate, clavate;
opercula low conical.
Fruit large, to 1.2 cm wide, globular; rims distal to widest
point; discs flat; valves flat.

CHAPTER 6 SINGLE-CAPPED EUCALYPTS

Red Stringybarks

Group characteristics
Bark stringybark.
Juvenile leaves alternate, petiolate, undulate; early ones rough.
Adult leaves falcate, concolourous; venation acute.
Inflorescences axillary, simple, pedunculate.
Buds non-scarred, in sevens or more.
Fruit medium to large, globular, discs wide, elevated; valves exsert.

Division of the Red Stringybarks into species
1 **Buds** pedicellate, clavate, opercula low conical or hemispherical.
    2 **Fruit** to 1.2 cm wide, rims at or distal to widest point,

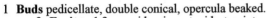

        E. laevopinea (Silvertop Stringybark): tall forest tree, found
north from Rylstone, New South Wales. Q
Bark sometimes gum on small branches.
Juvenile leaves broad-lanceolate, glossy, green.
Adult leaves lanceolate, dull, green.

1 **Buds** pedicellate, double conical, opercula beaked.
    2 **Fruit** to 1.2 cm wide, rims at widest point.

        E. macrorhyncha (Red stringybark): medium sized woodland
tree, found ranges and inland slopes, south from Warialda, New
South Wales; Gippsland, western, central, north-eastern
Victoria; Clare, South Australia.
Juvenile leaves broad-lanceolate to ovate, glossy, green.
Adult leaves lanceolate, dull to semi-glossy, green.

1 **Buds** pedicellate, double conical, angular, flared; opercula beaked.
    2 **Fruit** to 1.5 cm wide, rims flared, at widest point.

        E. cannonii (Capertree Red Stringybark): small tree, found
Rylestone-Capertree region, New South Wales.
Juvenile leaves broad-lanceolate to ovate, glossy, green.
Adult leaves lanceolate, dull to semi-glossy, green.

1 **Buds** shortly pedicellate, ovoid to fusiform, angular.
    2 **Fruit** to 1.3 cm wide; rims at widest point.
        3 **Adult leaves** lanceolate, dull to semi-glossy, green to blue-green.
        E. stannicola: medium sized tree, found from Torrington to
Tingha, New South Wales.
Juvenile leaves ovate, glossy, green.

1 **Buds** sessile, ovoid to fusiform, angular.
    2 **Fruit** to 1.5 cm wide; rims at widest point.
        3 **Adult leaves** lanceolate, semi-glossy to glossy, green.
        E. youmanii (Youman's stringybark): medium sized forest
tree, found from Guyra to Armidale, New South Wales.
Juvenile leaves broad-lanceolate to ovate, glossy, green.

1,   2 and 3 continued on next page.

3 **Adult leaves** broad-lanceolate, semi-glossy, green.
E. williamsiana (William's Stringybark): small tree, found eastern tableland, north from Niangala, New South Wales. Q
Juvenile leaves ovate to orbicular, glossy, green.

2 **Fruit** to 1.2 cm wide, rims at the widest point.
3 **Adult leaves** narrow-lanceolate to lanceolate, glossy to semi-glossy, green.
E. subtilior: medium sized tree, found Glen Innes to Stanthorpe, New South Wales. Q
Juvenile leaves broad-lanceolate, glossy, green.

1 **Buds** sessile to shortly pedicellate, fusiform.
2 **Fruit** to 1.2 cm wide, rims distal to widest point, discs raised; valves weakly exsert.

E. mckintii (East Gippsland Stringybark): a medium sized forest tree, found East Gippsland, Victoria.
Juvenile leaves ovate, semi-glossy, blue-green.
Adult leaves lanceolate to broad-lanceolate, semi-glossy, blue-green.

White Stringybark

Group characteristics
Bark stringybark.
Juvenile leaves alternate, petiolate, undulate, glossy, green; early ones rough.
Adult leaves falcate, oblique, concolourous to faintly discolourous, green to grey-green; venation acute.
Inflorescences axillary, simple, pedunculate.
Buds non-scarred, in sevens or more, sessile to shortly pedicellate, fusiform to ovoid.
Fruit globular to hemispherical; valves flat to weakly exsert.

Division of the White Stringybarks into species
1 **Buds** angular.
2 **Juvenile leaves** broad-lanceolate.

4 **Adult leaves** lanceolate to broad-lanceolate, semi-glossy.
E. prominula: medium sized tree found near Bucketty, New South Wales.
Fruit open (shortly pedicellate), medium sized, to 0.9 cm wide; discs wide, flat to weakly raised; rims distal to widest point.

1 continued on next page.

1 **Buds** round.
  2 **Juvenile leaves** broad-lanceolate to ovate.
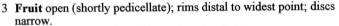
    3 **Fruit** crowded or open (sessile to shortly pedicellate), medium to large, to 1.1 cm wide; discs wide, raised; rims widest point or distal to widest point.
      4 **Adult leaves** lanceolate, glossy to semi-glossy.
        E. tindaliae (Tindale's Stringybark): medium sized forest tree, found north from Coffs Harbour, New South Wales. Q

    3 **Fruit** open (shortly pedicellate); rims distal to widest point; discs narrow.
      4 **Adult leaves** broad-lanceolate, semi-glossy.
        E. caliginosa (Broad-leaves Stringybark): medium sized tree, found north from Yarrowitch, Liverpool Range, New England Tableland , New South Wales. Q
        Bark coarsely furrowed.
        Fruit medium sized, to 0.7 cm wide; discs flat or raised.

      4 **Adult leaves** lanceolate, dull.
        E. eugenioides (Thin-leaved Stringybark) medium sized forest tree, found coast and nearby hills north from Wyndham, southern New South Wales. Q
        Fruit medium sized, to 0.9 cm wide; discs flat or raised.

    3 **Fruit** crowded (sessile or sub-sessile); rims distal to widest point; discs narrow.
      4 **Adult leaves** lanceolate to broad-lanceolate, glossy; shortest leaves about 6 cm long.
        5 Medium to tall forest tree, found escarpments, Yarras to Boonoo Boonoo, northern New South Wales.
        E. cameronii (Diehard Stringybark)
        Fruit small to medium sized, to 0.7 cm wide; discs depressed

      4 **Adult leaves** lanceolate to broad-lanceolate, glossy; shortest leaves >6 cm long.

        5 Medium sized forest tree, found coast and nearby hills; New South Wales, eastern Victoria.
          6 **Fruit** medium sized, to 0.9 cm wide; discs flat.
          E. globoidea (White Stringybark)
          South from Woolgoolga, New South Wales

2,   4,   5 and 6 continued on next page.

6 **Fruit** medium sized, to 0.9 cm wide; discs descending.
E. yangoura (Southern White Stringybark)
South from Cobargo, New South Wales.

5 Small tree, found on poor sandy soil on sandstone, Gosford to Yerrinbool and lower Blue Mountains, central coast and nearby hills, New South Wales.
E. oblonga
Fruit medium sized, to 0.9 cm wide; discs flat to raised.

4 **Adult leaves** broad-lanceolate to ovate, glossy.
5 Small tree, found east of Nowra, New South Wales.
E. imitans
Fruit medium sized, to 0.9 cm wide; discs flat to slightly raised.

4 **Adult leaves** lanceolate, glossy, erect; shortest leaves <6 cm long.
5 Mallee to small tree, found Blue Mountains, south of Sydney, Gibraltar Range National Park, New South Wales.
E. ligustrina (Privet Leaved Stringybark)
Bark is loosely latticed.
Fruit small, to 0.5 cm wide; discs depressed or flat.

2 **Juvenile leaves** linear to lanceolate.

3 **Fruit** open (shortly pedicellate), medium sized, to 0.8 cm wide; rims distal to widest point; discs narrow, flat or raised.
4 **Adult leaves** lanceolate, glossy.
6 Medium sized tree, found Murrurundi, New South Wales.
E. conjuncta

3 **Fruits** crowded to weakly open, shortly pedicellate, medium sized, to 0.7 cm long; rims distal to widest point; discs flat; valves flat.
4 **Adult leaves** lanceolate, glossy.
5 Medium sized tree, found from Tingha to Bendemeer, New England Tableland, New South Wales.
E. mckieana (McKie's Stringybark)

3 **Fruit** crowded (sub-sessile); rims distal to widest point; discs narrow.
4 **Adult leaves** narrow-lanceolate to lanceolate, glossy.

5 Medium sized tree, found from Blue Mountains to Coonabarabran, New South Wales.
E. sparsifolia (Narrow-leaved Stringybark)
Fruit medium sized, to 0.8 cm wide; discs flat to raised.

4 continued on next page.

4 **Adult leaves** narrow-lanceolate, dull; shortest leaves <6 cm long.
    5 Medium sized tree, found Rylestone-Capertree region of New South Wales.
    E. tenella (Capertree White Stringybark)
    Fruit medium sized, to 0.7 cm wide; discs flat.

4 **Adult leaves** linear to narrow-lanceolate, glossy; shortest leaves >6 cm long.
    5 Medium sized tree, found Yalwal near Nowra, New South Wales.
    E. ralla
    Fruit medium sized, to 0.7 cm wide; discs flat raised.

Brown Stringybarks

Group characteristics
Bark stringybark.
Juvenile leaves alternate, petiolate; early ones rough.
Adult leaves falcate, oblique, concolourous; venation acute.
Inflorescences axillary, simple, pedunculate.
Buds non-scarred, in sevens or more, sessile.

Division of the Brown Stringybarks into species
1 **Fruit** globular, wider than long; rims distal to widest point; discs slightly elevated; valves flat or weakly exsert.
    2 **Buds** fusiform; opercula high conical.
    E. agglomerata (Blue-leaved Stringybark): medium tall forest tree, found central tableland, central and southern coast, New South Wales, and just into Victoria.
    Juvenile leaves broad-lanceolate, glossy, green.
    Adult leaves lanceolate to broad-lanceolate, glossy to semi-glossy, grey-green.
    Fruit medium sized, to 1 cm wide, compressed.

    2 **Buds** ovoid, opercula low conical, angular.
        3 **Juvenile leaves** orbicular, cordate, glossy, green; petioles short.
        E. camfieldii (Camfield's Stringybark): mallee to small tree, found Gosford to Royal National Park, New South Wales.
        Adult leaves broad-lanceolate, glossy, green, leathery.
        Fruit medium sized, to 0.9 cm wide.

        3 **Juvenile leaves** ovate, dull, grey-green.
        E. bensonii: small tree, found on Army Trail, Wollemi National Park, New South Wales.
        Adult leaves broad-lanceolate to ovate, glossy, green, leathery.
        Fruit medium sized, to 1 cm wide.

1 and 2 continued on next page.

2 **Buds** fusiform; opercula high conical, angular.

E. capitellata (Brown Stringybark): mallee to small tree, found Karuah to Nowra, central coast New South Wales.
Juvenile leaves broad-lanceolate, glossy, green.
Adult leaves lanceolate to broad-lanceolate, glossy, green.
Fruit large, to 1.2 cm wide.

2 **Buds** ovoid; opercula low conical, warty.

   3 **Juvenile leaves** orbicular to ovate, glossy, green.

E. baxteri (Brown Stringybark): mallee to tall tree, found southern Victoria; just into south coast New South Wales; south-eastern coast South Australia.
Adult leaves broad-lanceolate, glossy, green, leathery.
Fruit large, to 1.6 cm wide.

2 **Buds** ovoid; opercula low conical, slightly warty.

   3 **Juvenile leaves** broad-lanceolate, glossy, green.

E. arenacea (Brown Stringybark): mallee to small tree, found Little Desert, Victoria, and into South Australia.
Adult leaves broad-lanceolate, glossy, green, leathery.
Fruit medium sized, to 1 cm wide.

1 **Fruit** globular; rims distal to widest point; discs wide, slightly raised; valves exsert.

  2 **Buds** clavate; opercula hemispherical to low conical.

E. blaxlandii (Blaxland's Stringybark): small to medium sized forest tree, found central tableland and southern ranges, New South Wales.
Juvenile leaves broad-lanceolate, glossy, green; roughness on under surface only.
Adult leaves broad-lanceolate, dull, green.
Fruit large, to 1.3 cm wide.

Mongamulla Gum

E. deuaensis (Mongamulla Gum): mallee, found on cliff face near Mount Mongamulla, Deua National Park, New South Wales.
Bark gum.
Juvenile leaves subopposite, shortly petiolate, broad-lanceolate, glossy, green; early ones rough.
Adult leaves lanceolate, glossy, green, erect, concolourous; venation acute.

Inflorescences axillary, simple, non-pedunculate.
Buds non-scarred, in sevens, sessile, double conical, angular.
Fruit large, to 1.4 cm wide, hemispherical; discs wide, raised; valves exsert.

Grampians Gums

E. alpina (Grampians Gum, eastern form): mallee, found Mount William and Serra Ranges, Grampians National Park, Victoria.
Bark box on trunk.
Juvenile leaves alternate, petiolate, orbicular, glossy, green, leathery, early ones rough.

Adult leaves ovate, falcate, oblique, glossy, green, falcate, oblique, concolourous, leathery; venation acute.
Inflorescences axillary, simple, non-pedunculate to very shortly pedunculate.
Buds non-scarred, in sevens or more, sessile, ovoid, very warty.
Fruit large, to 1.8 cm wide, hemispherical, warty; discs broad; valves exsert.

E. alpina (Grampians Gum, western form): small tree, found Victoria Range, Grampians National Park, Victoria.
Bark stringybark, on the trunk.
Juvenile leaves alternate, petiolate, orbicular, glossy, green, concolourous, early ones rough.

Adult leaves broad-lanceolate, falcate, oblique, glossy, green, leathery; venation acute.
Inflorescences axillary, simple, non-pedunculate to very shortly pedunculate.
Buds non-scarred, in sevens or more, sessile, ovoid, very warty.
Fruit large, to 1.5 cm wide, globular, warty; discs wide, slightly elevated; rims distal to the wides point; valves exsert.

Woila Gum

E. olsenii (Woila Gum): small tree, found only on ridges near Mother Woila, Deua National Park, New South Wales.
Bark compact, basal.
Juvenile leaves subopposite to alternate, petiolate, broad-lanceolate, glossy, green; early ones rough.

Adult leaves lanceolate, glossy, green, concolourous; venation acute.
Inflorescences axillary, simple, pedunculate.
Buds non-scarred, in sevens, sessile to shortly pedicellate, fusiform, ribbed.
Fruit extra large, to 2 cm long, ovoid, ribbed; discs depressed; rims thick.

BLACKBUTTS

Group characteristics
Bark stringybark, less furrowed than usual, medium length fibres.
Juvenile leaves opposite, sessile, broad lanceolate, dull, green, on square stems.
Adult leaves lanceolate, falcate, glossy, green, concolourous; venation acute.

Inflorescences axillary, simple, pedunculate.
Buds non-scarred, in sevens, pedicellate, ovoid to double conical, opercula conical, beaked.
Fruit globular to hemispherical, discs flat or depressed; rims thick.

Division of the Blackbutts into species.
1　**Fruit** medium to large, to 1.1 cm wide.
　　2　**Buds**, young **branches** green.
　　　　E. pilularis (Blackbutt): medium to very tall forest tree, found on sandy loams, coast, north from Eden, New South Wales. Q
　　　　Bark rough, to mid trunk.

1　**Fruit** large, to 1.7 cm wide.
　　2　**Buds**, young **branches** subglaucous to glaucous.
　　　　E. pyrocarpa (Large-fruited Blackbutt): medium to tall forest tree, found from Washpool to Wauchope, northern New South Wales.
　　　　Bark rough, to large branches.

CHAPTER 6 SINGLE-CAPPED EUCALYPTS

PEPPERMINTS

Division of the Peppermints
1 Trees; **bark** peppermint.
   Peppermint-barked Peppermint. page 107

1 Trees; **bark** basal, compact.
   E. elata (River Peppermint). page 109

1 Trees; **bark** gum.
   Gum-barked Peppermint. page 110

1 Mallees; **bark** gum; **buds, leaves** glaucous.
   Gum-barked Peppermint. page 110

1 Mallees; **bark** gum or peppermint; **buds, leaves** non-glaucous.
   Peppermint-barked Peppermint. page 107

Peppermint-barked Peppermints

Group characteristics
Bark peppermint.
Adult leaves concolourous; venation acute.
Inflorescences axillary, simple, pedunculate.
Buds non-scarred, in sevens or more, pedicellate, clavate.
Fruit cupular to pyriform; discs flat; valves flat.

Division of the Peppermint Barked Peppermints into species
1 **Bark** peppermint, to large branches or higher.
    2 **Juvenile leaves** opposite, sessile, broad-lanceolate or narrower, dull.
        3 **Adult leaves** narrow-lanceolate to lanceolate, semi-glossy to glossy, green.
            4 **Buds** green; opercula low conical.
               E. radiata (Narrow-leaved Peppermint)
               Fruit small to 0.6 cm long.
               5 **Juvenile leaves** narrow-lanceolate, green.
                  ssp. radiata: wide spread small to medium sized tree, found central and southern tablelands and southern coast, New South Wales.

               5 **Juvenile leaves** broad lanceolate, green.
                  ssp. sejuncta: small to medium sized tree, found northern tablelands, New South Wales.

               5 **Juvenile leaves** lanceolate to broad-lanceolate, green.
                  subspecies: small to medium sized tree, found central and southern Victoria, and Lemonthyme region, Tasmania.

1,   2,   3 and 4 continued on next page.

4 **Buds** green; opercula high conical.
  5 **Juvenile leaves** narrow-lanceolate, green.
    subspecies: medium sized tree, found north of Dividing Range, east of Melbourne.

3 **Adult leaves** narrow-lanceolate to lanceolate, dull, grey-green to sub-glaucous.
  4 **Buds** glaucous; opercula conical to high conical.
    E. robertsonii (Narrow-leaved Peppermint)
    Fruit small, to 0.6 cm long.
      5 **Juvenile leaves** narrow-lanceolate, grey-green.
        6 **Opercula** high conical.
          ssp. robertsonii: a medium to tall tree, found on ranges; south-eastern New South Wales, north-eastern Victoria.
          Adult leaves narrow-lanceolate.

      5 **Juvenile leaves** lanceolate, grey-green.
        6 **Opercula** conical.
          ssp. hemispherica: medium sized tree, found near Orange, New South Wales.
          Adult leaves lanceolate.

  4 **Buds** glaucous; opercula conical to low conical.

      5 **Juvenile leaves** lanceolate to broad-lanceolate, grey-green to glaucous.
        E. croajingolensis (East Gippsland Peppermint): small tree, found coast and nearby hills; eastern Victoria, southern New South Wales.
        Fruit small, to 0.6 cm long.

2 **Juvenile leaves** opposite, sessile, broad-lanceolate to ovate, cordate, dull, green.
  3 **Adult leaves** narrow-lanceolate to lanceolate, semi-glossy, green.
    E. willisii ssp. willisii (Shining Peppermint): mallee to small tree, found on coast, Victoria, and into south-eastern South Australia..
    Fruit small, to 0.5 cm long.

2 **Juvenile leaves** ovate, grey-green to glaucous, some connate.
  3 **Adult leaves** lanceolate to broad-lanceolate, glossy, green.
    E. dives (Broad-leaved Peppermint): small to medium sized tree, found mountains; central and southern New South Wales, central and eastern Victoria.
    Fruit medium sized, to 0.7 cm long.

1 and 2 continued on next page.

2 **Juvenile leaves** at first opposite, sessile; then alternate, petiolate, narrow-lanceolate, dull, grey-green.

3 **Adult leaves** narrow-lanceolate to lanceolate, dull, grey-green.
E. amygdalina (Black Peppermint): a small to medium sized tree, found widespread north-central and eastern Tasmania.
Fruit medium sized, to 0.7 cm long.

1 **Bark**; mallees basal; trees mid to high trunk.

2 **Juvenile leaves** opposite, sessile, broad-lanceolate to ovate, dull, grey-green.

3 **Adult leaves** narrow-lanceolate to lanceolate, dull, green.
E. nitida (Smithton Peppermint): mallee to small tree, found northern, western and southern Tasmania.
Fruit medium sized, to 0.8 cm long.

2 **Juvenile leaves** at first opposite, sessile; then alternate, petiolate, broad-lanceolate, falcate, dull, grey-green.

3 **Adult leaves** narrow-lanceolate to lanceolate, dull green.
E. willisii ssp. falciformis (Grampians Peppermint): mallee to small tree, found Grampians National Park, Victoria.
Fruit medium sized to 0.7 cm long.

Compact-barked Peppermint

E. elata (River Peppermint) medium to tall forest tree, found central tableland and southern coast, south from Putty, New South Wales; eastern Victoria.
Bark compact, basal.
Juvenile leaves opposite, sessile, lanceolate, dull, green.
Adult leaves narrow-lanceolate, glossy, green, concolourous; venation acute.
Inflorescences axillary, simple, pedunculate.
Buds non-scarred, in twenties or more, pedicellate, clavate.
Fruit small, to 0.6 cm long, globular; discs flat to depressed; valves flat.

CHAPTER 6 SINGLE-CAPPED EUCALYPTS

Gum-bark Peppermints

Group characteristics
All found in Tasmania.
Bark gum.
Adult leaves concolourous, dull; venation acute.

Inflorescences axillary, simple, pedunculate.
Buds non-scarred, pedicellate, clavate.
Fruit; discs flat; valves flat.

Division of the Gum Barked Peppermints into species

1 **Adult leaves** linear, green or grey-green.
    2 **Fruit** small to medium sized, to 0.7 cm wide, hemispherical to pyriform.
        E. pulchella (White Peppermint): small to medium sized tree, found
        south-eastern Tasmania.
        Juvenile leaves opposite, sessile, becoming alternate, petiolate,
        linear to narrow-lanceolate, dull, green.
        Buds in elevens or more.

1 **Adult leaves** rarely formed, maturing as **juvenile leaves**.
    2 **Fruit** medium sized, to 0.9 cm wide, glaucous, hemispherical to pyriform.
        E. risdonii (Risdon Peppermint): mallee to small tree, found near Risdon,
        Tasmania.
        Buds in sevens or more, glaucous.
        Juvenile leaves opposite, sessile, ovate to orbicular, sometimes connate,
        glaucous.

1 **Adult leaves** broad-lanceolate, grey-green to glaucous.
    2 **Fruit** medium to large, to 1.1 cm wide, hemispherical to pyriform.
        E. tenuiramis (Silver Peppermint): small to medium sized tree, found
        south-eastern Tasmania.
        Juvenile leaves ovate, sometimes connate, glaucous.
        Buds sevens or more, glaucous.

    2 **Fruit** large, to 1.3 cm wide, hemispherical, often glaucous, often angles;
    discs flat, red.
    E. coccifera (Tasmanian Snow Gum): small tree, found high altitudes,
    Tasmania.
    Juvenile leaves orbicular to ovate, dull, blue-green; stems red, glaucous.
        Buds in threes or sevens, wrinkled, angular, glaucous; opercula
        flat, very warty.

CHAPTER 6 SINGLE-CAPPED EUCALYPTS

ASHES

The Ashes can be divided into groups.

Green-leaved Ashes (page 112) have glossy and green juvenile leaves.
  Including **Mallees Ashes (page 113)**

Black Sallies (page 116) have stellate clustered buds and small globular fruit.

Blue-leaved Ashes have dull and grey-green or glaucous juvenile leaves.
  Narrow-flowered Blue-leaved Ashes (page 117) all stamens have anthers.
    Including **Snow Gums and White Sallies (page 118)** with parallel venation.

  Broad-flowered Blue-leaved Ashes (page 120) have staminodes.
    Including **Scribbly Gums (page 122)** with gum bark

Division of the Ashes (excluding Black Sallies)
1 **Juvenile leaves** glossy, green.
      3 Mainly **Mallees**.

          5 **Fruit** large, 1-1.3 cm long, cupular, ribbed; discs flat.
            E. luehmanniana (Yellow-topped Mallee Ash)
                        (page 118) NSW
          5 **Fruit** not as above.
            Mallee Ash (page 113) NSW VIC

      3 Mainly **Trees**.
        Green-leaved Ash (page 112) NSW VIC SA TAS

1 **Juvenile leaves** dull, grey-green or glaucous.
    2 **Adult leaves**; venation parallel.
    Snow Gum (page 118) NSW VIC SA TAS

    2 **Adult leaves**; venation acute or not visible.
      3 Mainly **mallees**.

          5 **Fruit** medium sized to 0.7 cm long, ovoid to slightly
            urceolate; discs descending; rims thin.
            E. cunninghamii (Cliff Mallee Ash) (page 114) NSW

          5 **Fruit** medium sized, to 0.8 cm wide, pyriform or
            hemispherical; discs flat.
            Broad-flowered Blue-leaved Ash (page 120) NSW SA

      3 Mainly **trees**.
        4 **Bark** gum.
          Scribbly Gum (page 122) NSW

        4 **Bark** stringybark.
          Narrow-flowered Blue-leaved Ash (page 117) NSW VIC
                          TAS

        4 continued on next page.

4 **Bark** peppermint.
    5 **Fruit** ovoid or urceolate.
       E. piperita (Sydney Peppermint) (page 117) NSW

    5 **Fruit** hemispherical to pyriform.
       Broad-flowered Blue-leaved Ash (page 120) NSW
                                     VIC

4 **Bark** compact, basal.
    5 **Fruit** globular; opening small.
       E. stenostoma (Jillaga Ash) (page 121) NSW

    5 **Fruit** cylindrical or globular to urceolate; opening wide.
       Narrow-flowered Blue-leaved Ash (page 117) NSW
                                       VIC

4 **Bark** compact or ironbark, to large branches.
    E. sieberi (Silvertop Ash) (page 121) NSW VIC TAS

Green-leaved Ashes

Group characteristics
Juvenile leaves alternate, petiolate, glossy, green.
Adult leaves oblique, glossy, green; venation acute.
Inflorescences pedunculate.
Buds non-scarred; stamens all have anthers.

Division of the Green-leaved Ashes into species
1 **Buds** in sevens or more, pedicellate, clavate; opercula low conical.
    2 **Inflorescences** axillary, paired.
        3 **Bark** peppermint, on lower trunk.

           4 **Fruit** medium sized, to 0.9 cm long, pyriform; discs flat to slightly depressed; valves flat to slightly exsert.
           E. regnans (Mountain Ash): very tall forest tree, found mountains; southern Victoria, Tasmania.
           Juvenile leaves ovate.
           Adult leaves lanceolate to broad-lanceolate, concolourous.

        3 **Bark** stringybark, less furrowed than usual, medium length fibres, to large branches
           4 **Fruit** medium sized, to 0.9 cm long, pyriform; discs flat to slightly raised; valves flat to slightly exsert.
           E. fastigata (Brown Barrel): tall to very tall forest tree, found tablelands and escarpments, south from Ebor, New South Wales, and into eastern Victoria.
           Juvenile leaves broad-lanceolate to ovate.
           Adult leaves lanceolate, concolourous or discolourous.

1 and 2 continued on next page.

2 **Inflorescences** axillary, simple.
  3 **Bark** stringybark, less furrowed than usual, medium length fibres, on trunk or to large branches
    4 **Fruit** medium to large, to 1.1 cm long, ovoid to slightly urceolate; discs depressed.

E. obliqua (Messmate or Messmate Stringybark): small to very tall forest tree, found widely; eastern New South Wales, southern Victoria, southern South Australia, Tasmania. Q
Juvenile leaves ovate.
Adult leaves broad-lanceolate, very oblique, concolourous.

  3 **Bark** compact, basal.
    4 **Fruit** small, to 0.6 cm long, globular; discs depressed.
      E. paliformis (Wadbilliga Ash): small tree, found Mount Wadbilliga, Wadbilliga National Park, New South Wales.
      Juvenile leaves lanceolate.
      Adult leaves lanceolate, concolourous.

    4 **Fruit** medium to large, to 1.1 cm long, ovoid to slightly urceolate; discs depressed.
      E. dendromorpha (Budawang Ash): small tree, found localised areas, Mount Tomah to Monga, southern tableland New South Wales.
      Juvenile leaves broad-lanceolate.
      Adult leaves lanceolate, concolourous.

1 **Buds** in threes, sessile; hypanthia cylindrical; opercula hemispherical, warty.
  2 **Inflorescences** axillary, simple.
    3 **Bark** compact, basal.
      4 **Fruit** medium sized, to 1 cm long, cupular to urceolate; discs depressed.

E. triflora (Pigeon House Ash): mallee to small tree, found on sandstone escarpments, Pigeon House Mountain to Nerringa, New South Wales.
Juvenile leaves broad-lanceolate.
Adult leaves lanceolate, concolourous.

Mallee Ashes (Green-leaved Ashes)

Group characteristics
Mallees.
Bark gum.
Juvenile leaves alternate, petiolate.
Adult leaves glossy, green, concolourous, often partially erect; venation acute or not visible.
Inflorescences axillary, simple, pedunculate.
Buds non-scarred; stamens all have anthers.
Integration occurs between these species.

Division of the Mallee Ashes into species

1 **Buds** in sevens.
    2 **Buds** pedicellate, clavate; opercula hemispherical, pointed, warty.
        3 **Fruit** ovoid to slightly urceolate; discs descending; rims thin.
            4 **Fruit** medium to large, to 1.2 cm long.
                5 **Adult leaves** broad-lanceolate to ovate, to 2.5 cm wide, leathery.
                E. obstans (Port Jackson Mallee): found Kuringai Chase to Jervis Bay, New South Wales.
                Juvenile leaves broad-lanceolate to ovate, glossy, green.

                5 **Adult leaves** lanceolate to broad-lanceolate, to 3.5 cm wide.
                E. burgessiana (Faulconbridge Mallee Ash): found near Faulconbridge, Blue Mountains, New South Wales.
                Juvenile leaves broad-lanceolate to ovate, glossy, green.

            4 **Fruit** medium to large, to 1.1 cm long.
                5 **Adult leaves** lanceolate, to 2 cm wide.
                E. spectatrix: found on several mountain tops, near Bega, New South Wales.
                Juvenile leaves broad-lanceolate, glossy, green.

                5 **Adult leaves** linear to narrow-lanceolate, to 0.7 cm wide.
                E. laophila: found from Rylstone to Newnes, New South Wales.
                Juvenile leaves narrow-lanceolate to lanceolate, glossy, green.

            4 **Fruit** medium sized, to 1 cm long.
                5 **Adult leaves** narrow-lanceolate to lanceolate to 1 cm wide.
                E. stricta (Blue Mountains Mallee Ash): found Newnes Plateau to Budawang National Park, New South Wales.
                Juvenile leaves broad-lanceolate, glossy, green.

            4 **Fruit** medium sized, to 0.9 cm long.
                5 **Adult leaves** linear to narrow-lanceolate, to 0.7 cm wide.
                E. apiculata: found from Linden to Berrima, New South Wales.
                Juvenile leaves narrow-lanceolate, glossy, green.

            4 **Fruit** medium sized, to 0.7 cm long.
                5 **Adult leaves** narrow-lanceolate to 0.8 cm wide; tips pinkish-grey.
                E. cunninghamii (Cliff Mallee Ash): found on cliff tops, Blue Mountains, New South Wales.
                Juvenile leaves narrow-lanceolate, dull, grey-green.

1,   2,   3 continued on next page.

3 **Fruit** cupular to slightly urceolate; discs flat to depressed; rims thick.
    4 **Fruit** medium sized, to 0.8 cm long.

        5 **Adult leaves** narrow-lanceolate, to 0.9 cm wide.
          E. approximans (Barren Mountain Mallee): found on a granite hillside, Barren Mountain, New England National Park, New South Wales.
          Juvenile leaves lanceolate, glossy, green.

        5 **Adult leaves** lanceolate to broad-lanceolate, to 1.6 cm wide.
          E. microcodon: found Mount Glennie, northern New South Wales. Q
          Juvenile leaves lanceolate, glossy, green.

2 **Buds** sessile to shortly pedicellate, cylindrical, angular; opercula hemispherical, pointed, warty.
    3 **Fruit** ovoid to urceolate, discs descending.
        4 **Fruit** medium sized, to 1 cm long.
          5 **Adult leaves** lanceolate; stems square.
          E. langleyi: found in isolated spots near Nowra, New South Wales.
          Juvenile leaves broad-lanceolate to ovate, glossy, green.

2 **Buds** sessile, clavate; opercula hemispherical, pointed, warty.
    3 **Fruit** hemispherical; discs flat to weakly raised; valves flat.
        4 **Fruit** medium sized, to 0.8 cm wide.
          5 **Adult leaves** lanceolate to 1.5 cm wide.
          E. kybeanensis (Kybean Mallee Ash): found at high altitudes; south from Kybean, New South Wales, eastern Victoria.
          Juvenile leaves lanceolate, glossy, green.

1 **Buds** often in threes.
    2 **Buds** sessile to subsessile, clavate; opercula hemispherical, pointed, warty.
        3 **Fruit** campanulate; discs flat; valves flat.
          4 **Fruit** medium sized, to 0.9 cm long.

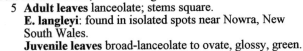

            5 **Adult leaves** lanceolate, to 1.8 cm wide.
             E. codonocarpa (Bell-fruited Mallee Ash): found on several isolated granite outcrops, north of Ebor, New South Wales. Q
             Juvenile leaves lanceolate, glossy, green.

CHAPTER 6 SINGLE-CAPPED EUCALYPTS

Black Sallies

Group characteristics

Adult leaves concolourous.
Inflorescences axillary, simple, pedunculate.
Buds non-scarred, in sevens or more, sessile, fusiform; opercula high conical, (stellate clusters); stamens all have anthers.
Fruit globular, crowded; discs depressed.

Division of the Black Sallies into species

1 **Bark** gum; small trees.
    2 **Adult leaves** narrow-lanceolate to lanceolate, glossy, green; venation acute.
        3 **Juvenile leaves** alternate, petiolate, lanceolate, glossy, green.
        E. mitchelliana (Mount Buffalo Sally): found Mt Buffalo, Victoria.
        Fruit small to medium sized, to 0.7 cm wide.

    2 **Adult leaves** lanceolate to broad-lanceolate, glossy, green; venation parallel.
        3 **Juvenile leaves** opposite, sessile, broad-lanceolate, dull, grey-green.
        E. copulans once found Wentworth falls, New South Wales.
        Fruit small, to 0.5 cm wide.

1 **Bark** compact, grey to black, lower half of trunk, olive green gum above; small trees.
    2 **Adult leaves** lanceolate to ovate, glossy, green; venation parallel.
        3 **Juvenile leaves** opposite, sessile, ovate to orbicular, dull, grey-green.
        E. stellulata (Black Sally): found in wet cold sites, subalpine regions; New South Wales, Victoria.
        Fruit small, to 0.5 cm wide.

1 **Bark** gum; mallees.
    2 **Adult leaves** narrow-lanceolate to lanceolate, <1 cm wide, to 7 cm long, dull, grey-green; venation parallel.
        3 **Juvenile leaves** opposite, sessile, narrow-lanceolate, dull, grey-green.
        E. moorei (Narrow-leaved Sally): found in isolated spots on sandstone tablelands, Blue Mountains, Budawang, Wadbilliga, Gibraltar Range and Snowy Mountains National Parks, New South Wales.
        Fruit small, to 0.4 cm wide.

    2 **Adult leaves** linear to narrow-lanceolate, <1 cm wide, to 12 cm long, glossy to semi-glossy, green; venation parallel.
        3 **Juvenile leaves** opposite, sessile, narrow-lanceolate, dull, grey-green.
        E. serpentinicola: found near Gloucester, New South Wales.
        Fruit small, to 0.5 cm wide.

    2 **Adult leaves** lanceolate to broad-lanceolate, >1 cm wide, glossy, green; venation parallel.
        3 **Juvenile leaves** opposite, sessile, broad-lanceolate, dull, grey-green.
        E. latiuscula: found Wadbilliga National Park, New South Wales.
        Fruit small, to 0.4 cm wide.

CHAPTER 6 SINGLE-CAPPED EUCALYPTS

Narrow-flowered Blue-leaved Ashes

Group characteristics
Juvenile leaves alternate, petiolate, vertical.
Adult leaves concolourous; venation acute.
Inflorescences axillary, simple, pedunculate.
Buds non-scarred, in sevens or more; stamens all have anthers.

Division of the Narrow-flowered Blue-leaved Ashes into species
1 **Fruit** medium sized, to 0.8 cm long, ovoid or to 0.9 cm long, urceolate; discs depressed.
    2 **Buds** pedicellate, fusiform.
        3 **Bark** peppermint, to large branches.

            E. piperita (Sydney Peppermint): a small to medium sized tree, found central to south coast and tableland, New South Wales.
            Juvenile leaves ovate, dull, grey-green.
            Adult leaves lanceolate to broad-lanceolate, dull, green to grey-green.

1 **Fruit** extra large, to 2.6 cm long, ovoid, ribbed; discs depressed; rims thick.
    2 **Buds** pedicellate, fusiform, ribbed.
        3 **Bark** fine patterned, spongy, prickly.

            E. planchoniana (Needlebark Stringybark) small to medium sized tree, found north coast, north from Laurieton, New South Wales. Q
            Juvenile leaves ovate, dull, grey-green.
            Adult leaves lanceolate to broad-lanceolate, glossy, grey-green.

1 **Fruit** large, to 1.5 cm wide, ovoid; discs depressed.
    2 **Buds** pedicellate, clavate.
        3 **Bark** stringybark, to mid trunk.
            4 **Juvenile leaves** broad-lanceolate to ovate, dull, grey-green.
            E. delegatensis ssp delegatensis(Alpine Ash): tall to very tall forest tree, found at high altitudes; south from Brindabella, New South Wales, east and central Victoria.
            Adult leaves lanceolate, glossy, green.

        3 **Bark** stringybark, to large branches.
            4 **Juvenile leaves** orbicular, dull, grey-green.
            E. delegatensis ssp. tasmaniensis (Gum-topped Stringybark): tall to very tall forest tree, found at high altitudes, Tasmania.
            Adult leaves lanceolate, glossy, green.

1 continued on next page.

1 **Fruit** medium sized, to 1.1 cm long, globular to slightly urceolate; discs depressed.
　　2 **Buds** pedicellate, ovoid to clavate,
　　　　3 **Bark** gum, basal compact.

E. fraxinoides (White Ash): medium to tall, forest tree, found ranges, south from Sassafras, New South Wales, and just into eastern Victoria..
Juvenile leaves broad-lanceolate, dull, grey-green.
Adult leaves narrow-lanceolate to lanceolate, glossy, green.

1 **Fruit** medium sized, to 1 cm long, ovoid; discs flat or depressed, wide.
　　2 **Buds** sessile to shortly pedicellate, to 0.2 cm long, clavate; opercula conical.
　　　　3 **Bark** gum, basal compact.

E. oreades (Blue Mountains Ash): small to medium sized forest tree, found Blue Mountains north from Mittagong and several isolated spots on northern New South Wales ranges. Q
Adult leaves lanceolate, semi-glossy, green.
Juvenile leaves ovate, dull, grey-green to glaucous.

1 **Fruit** are large, to 1.3 cm long, cupular, ribbed; discs flat, wide.
　　2 **Buds** pedicellate, fusiform, ribbed, yellow.
　　　　2 **Bark** gum.

E. luehmanniana (Yellow-topped Mallee Ash): mallee, found Kariong to Bulli, central coast New South Wales.
Adult leaves lanceolate to broad-lanceolate, glossy, green; young stems yellow, square.
Juvenile leaves broad-lanceolate, glossy, green.

Snow Gums and Sallies (Narrow-flowered Blue-leaved Ashes)

Group characteristics
Bark gum.
Juvenile leaves alternate, petiolate, dull, vertical.
Adult leaves concolourous; venation parallel.
Inflorescences axillary, simple, pedunculate.
Buds non-scarred, in sevens or more, sessile to shortly pedicellate, clavate; opercula low conical; stamens all have anthers.
Fruit pyriform; discs flat to slightly raised; valves flat.

Division of the Snow Gums into species
1 **Buds** round, green.
　　2 Small trees.

E. pauciflora (Snow Gum or White Sally): found mountain tops and tablelands; New South Wales, Victoria, Tasmania; several coastal regions, south New South Wales, around Western Port Bay, Victoria, Mount Gambia, South Australia, Tasmania. Q
Juvenile leaves ovate, grey-green.
Adult leaves lanceolate, glossy, green.
Fruit medium sized, to 1 cm wide.

1 and 2 continued on next page.

2 Mallees to small trees.

      5 Blue Mountains, Buderwang and Wadbilliga National Parks, New South Wales.
E. gregsoniana (Mallee Snow Gum):
Juvenile leaves lanceolate to broad-lanceolate, grey-green.
Adult leaves lanceolate, glossy, grey-green.
Fruit medium sized, to 0.8 cm wide.

      5 Baw Baw Plateau, Mount Useful, Victoria.
E. acerina (Snow Gum):
Juvenile leaves lanceolate to broad-lanceolate, grey-green.
Adult leaves lanceolate, glossy, grey-green.
Fruit medium sized, to 0.8 cm wide.

1 **Buds** round, glaucous.
   3 **Adult leaves** spacing <3 cm apart.

E. niphophila (Snow Gum): small tree or mallee, found alpine regions; southern New South Wales, Victoria.
Juvenile leaves broad-lanceolate to ovate, dull, grey-green, glaucous.
Adult leaves lanceolate to ovate, glossy, green or glaucous.
Fruit medium to large, to 1 cm wide.

   3 **Adult leaves** spacing >3 cm apart.
E. lacrimans: small tree, found near Adaminaby, New South Wales.
Juvenile leaves broad-lanceolate to ovate, dull, grey-green to glaucous.
Adult leaves lanceolate, glossy, green to grey-green.
Fruit medium to large, to 1.2 cm wide.

1 **Buds** round to some times angles, glaucous.
   3 **Adult leaves** spacing <3 cm apart.
     4 **Fruit** large, to 1.6 cm wide, some angles, base hemispherical.
E. hedraia (Snow Gum): small tree or mallee, found Falls Creek, Victoria.
Juvenile leaves broad-lanceolate, dull, grey-green to glaucous.
Adult leaves lanceolate, dull, grey-green.

1 **Buds** angles, glaucous.
   3 **Adult leaves** spacing <3 cm apart.
     4 **Fruit** large, to 1.4 cm wide, angles, base tapered.
E. debeuzevillei (Snow Gum): small tree or mallee, found Snowy Mountains, southern New South Wales.
Juvenile leaves broad-lanceolate, dull, grey-green to glaucous.
Adult leaves lanceolate, dull, grey-green.

ADDENDUM:
*After the printing of this Book **E. acerina** and **E. hedraia** were downgraded to variants of **E. pauciflora** and **E. niphophila** respectively.*

CHAPTER 6 SINGLE-CAPPED EUCALYPTS

Broad-flowered Blue-leaved Ashes

Group characteristics
Juvenile leaves alternate, petiolate, broad lanceolate to ovate, vertical, dull.
> **Adult leaves** lanceolate, concolourous, glossy; venation acute.
> **Inflorescences** axillary, simple, pedunculate.
> **Buds** non-scarred, in sevens or more, pedicellate, clavate; staminodes present.

Division of the Broad-flowered Blue-leaved Ashes into species
1 **Bark** peppermint, to at least large branches; medium to tall trees.
> 2 **Fruit** small, to 0.6 cm wide, hemispherical to slightly pyriform; discs flat; valves flat; length about equal to width.
> > **E. andrewsii (New England blackbutt)**: forest tree, found north from Niangala district, New England tablelands, New South Wales. Q
> > **Juvenile leaves** grey-green.
> > **Adult leaves** green.
> > **Buds** subglaucous.

> 2 **Fruit** small, to 0.6 cm wide, conical to slightly pyriform; discs flat; valves flat; length greater than width.
> > **E. campanulata (New England blackbutt)**: forest tree, found on escarpments, north from Barrington Tops National Park, New South Wales. Q
> > **Juvenile leaves** grey-green.
> > **Adult leaves** green.

> 2 **Fruit** medium sized, to 0.8 cm wide, pyriform; discs flat; valves flat.
> > 3 Timbarra Plateau to Gibraltar Range National Park, New South Wales.
> > **E. olida**
> > **Juvenile leaves** grey-green.
> > **Adult leaves** green.

> > 3 forest tree, found coast and nearby ranges; south from Rylstone, New South Wales, eastern Victoria
> > **E. consideniana (Yertchuk)**
> > **Juvenile leaves** grey-green.
> > **Adult leaves** green to grey-green.

1 **Bark** box, lower trunk; mallees.
> 2 **Fruit** medium sized, to 0.8 cm wide, hemispherical; discs flat; valves flat.
> > **E. remota (Kangaroo Island Mallee Ash)**: found west end, Kangaroo Island, South Australia.
> > **Juvenile leaves** grey-green.
> > **Adult leaves** grey-green.

1 continued on next page.

1 **Bark** ironbark (compact when young), to the large branches, white gum above; medium to tall trees;
　　2 **Fruit** medium sized, to 0.9 cm wide, pyriform; discs flat; valves flat, three.
　　　E. sieberi (Silvertop Ash): forest tree, found coast and tableland; south from Morisset, New South Wales, eastern Victoria, west of Melbourne, north-west, Tasmania.
　　　Juvenile leaves grey-green.
　　　Young branches glaucous.
　　　Adult leaves green.

1 **Bark** gum; mallees.
　　2 **Fruit** medium sized, to 0.8 cm wide, pyriform; discs flat; valves flat.
　　　E. multicaulis (Whipstick Mallee Ash): found Blue Mountains, New South Wales.
　　　Juvenile leaves grey-green.
　　　Adult leaves green.

1 **Bark** gum, basal compact; small leaning trees.
　　2 **Fruit** medium sized, to 1 cm wide, globular; discs depressed; opening small.
　　　E. stenostoma (Jillaga Ash): found several isolated ridge tops, Wadbilliga National Park, New South Wales.
　　　Juvenile leaves grey-green to glaucous.
　　　Adult leaves green.
　　　Buds glaucous.

CHAPTER 6 SINGLE-CAPPED EUCALYPTS

Scribbly Gums (Broad-flowered Blue-leaved Ashes)

Group characteristics
Bark gum, scribbles.
Juvenile leaves alternate, petiolate, dull, grey-green, vertical.
Adult leaves green, concolourous; venation acute.

Inflorescences axillary, simple, pedunculate.
Buds non-scarred, in more than sevens, pedicellate, clavate; staminodes present.
Fruit hemispherical to slightly pyriform; discs flat to slightly ascending; valves flat.

Division of the Scribbly Gums into species
1 **Fruit** medium sized, to 0.9 cm wide, discs often red.
  2 **Adult leaves** lanceolate to broad-lanceolate, glossy, green or grey-green, leathery, to 4 cm wide.
    3 Central coast and tableland, New South Wales.
    E. haemastoma (Scribbly Gum): small to medium sized tree.
    Juvenile leaves ovate.

1 **Fruit** small to medium sized, to 0.6 cm wide.
  2 **Adult leaves** lanceolate, glossy, green, leathery, to 4 cm wide.
    3 Central coast and tableland, south from Newcastle, New South Wales.
    E. sclerophylla (Scribbly Gum): small to medium sized tree.
    Juvenile leaves broad-lanceolate.

  2 **Adult leaves** lanceolate, glossy to semi-glossy, green, to 3 cm wide.
    3 Northern coast, north from Newcastle, New South Wales. Q
    E. signata (Scribbly Gum): small to tall tree.
    Juvenile leaves broad-lanceolate.

  2 **Adult leaves** narrow-lanceolate to lanceolate, dull, grey-green, to 1.5 cm wide.
    3 Central coast, New South Wales.
      4 **Opercula** conical
      E. racemosa (Snappy Gum or Scribbly Gum) small to medium sized tree.
      Juvenile leaves broad-lanceolate.

  2 **Adult leaves** narrow-lanceolate to lanceolate, dull, grey-green, to 1.3 cm wide.
    3 West of Dividing Range, Tenterfield to Bombala, New South Wales.
      4 **Opercula** hemispherical to weakly pointed.
      E. rossii (Scribbly Gum) small to medium sized tree.
      Juvenile leaves broad-lanceolate.

INDEX OF SCIENTIFIC NAMES

INDEX OF SCIENTIFIC NAMES

INDEX OF SCIENTIFIC NAMES

INDEX OF COMMON NAMES

INDEX OF COMMON NAMES

INDEX OF COMMON NAMES

INDEX OF COMMON NAMES

BIBLIOGRAPHY

Boland, D.J., Brooker, M.I.M., Chippendale, G.M., Hall N., Hyland, B.P.M., Johnston, R.D., Kleinig, D.A. & Turner, J.D. (1984) Forest Trees of Australia, Edn. 4 (Nelson/CSIRO, Canberra).

Boomsma, C.D. (1981) Native Trees of South Australia (Woods & Forest Department, South Australia).

Brooker, M.I.H. & Kleinig, D.A. (1983) Field Guide to Eucalypts South-eastern Australia (Inkata Press, Melbourne & Sydney).

Brooker, M.I.H. & Kleinig, D.A. (1990) Field Guide to Eucalypts South-western and Southern Australia (Inkata Press, Melbourne & Sydney).

Chippendale, G.M. (1968) Eucalyptus Buds and Fruits (Forestry and Timber Bureau, Canberra).

Chippendale, G.M. (1988) Flora of Australia Vol. 19 Myrtacea-Eucalypts, Angophora (Australian Government Publishing Service, Canberra).

Costermans, L.F. (1981) Native Trees and Shrubs of South-eastern Australia (Rigby, Adelaide).

Costermans, L.F. (1981) Trees of Victoria (Renwick Pride, Melbourne).

Hall, N. et al. (1971-79) Forest Tree Series Leaflets Nos.1-220 (Australian Government Publishing Services, Canberra & CSIRO, Melbourne).

Harden, G.J. (1991) Flora of New South Wales Vol 2 (New South Wales University Press).

Kelly, S. (1969) Eucalypts (Thomas Nelson, Australia).

Kelly, s. (1978) Eucalypts Vol. 2 (Thomas Nelson, Australia).

Kirkpatrick, J.B. & Blackhouse, S. An Illustrated Guide to Tasmanian Native Trees (Mercury-Walch, Tasmania).

Pryor, L.D., & Johnson, L.A.S. (1971) A Classification of the Eucalypts (Australian National University Press, Canberra).

Williams, J. (1972) New England Eucalypts (University of New England, Armidale).